Beats, Rhymes, and Classroom Life

||||||||||||||||||||||||||||||||||||||||||||||||||||||||||||||||||||||||||||||||||||||||||||||||||||||||||||||

HIP-HOP PEDAGOGY AND
THE POLITICS OF IDENTITY

||||||||||||||||||||||||||||||||||||||||||||||||||||||||||||||||||||||||||||||||||||||||||||||||||||||||||||||

Beats, Rhymes, and Classroom Life

HIP-HOP PEDAGOGY AND THE POLITICS OF IDENTITY

Marc Lamont Hill

Foreword by Gloria Ladson-Billings

Teachers College, Columbia University
New York and London

Published by Teachers College Press, 1234 Amsterdam Avenue, New York, NY 10027

Copyright © 2009 by Teachers College, Columbia University

See page xiv for credits/permissions acknowledgments section.

Library of Congress Cataloging-in-Publication Data

Hill, Marc Lamont.
    Beats, rhymes, and classroom life : hip-hop pedagogy and the politics of identity / Marc Lamont Hill ; foreword by Gloria Ladson-Billings.
    p. cm.
Includes bibliographical references and index.
ISBN 978-0-8077-4960-9 (pbk. : alk. paper)
ISBN 978-0-8077-4961-6 (hardcover : alk. paper)
    1. Education, Urban—United States—Sociological aspects. 2. Hip-hop—United States—Influence. 3. Literature—Study and teaching (Secondary)—United States. I. Title.
LC5131.H45 2009
370.9173′2—dc22   2008054819

ISBN 978-0-8077-4960-9 (paper)
ISBN 978-0-8077-4961-6 (hardcover)

Printed on acid-free paper
Manufactured in the United States of America

16   15   14   13   12   11   10   09   8   7   6   5   4   3   2   1

Contents

Foreword

I must confess that I initially did not greet the task of writing this Foreword with much enthusiasm. It arrived on my desk at a very bad time. I was knee-deep in responsibilities as a new department chair; I was already past deadline on several of my own writing tasks; I was on the road every weekend for the past 3 months; we were in the middle of one of the most exciting national presidential races in my lifetime; and I was involved in state-level education policy formation for the presidential campaign. No, I had no time to read another manuscript or write another Foreword.

However, one evening after a long day at work I crawled into bed and began reading Marc Lamont Hill's powerful text and knew I had no choice but to write its Foreword. For those who know me, there might be some thought that I am reinforcing my "Philly Connection" with young Dr. Hill. While that is a logical conclusion to which to jump, it would be incorrect. As I read Marc Lamont Hill's opening words about his growing up in Philadelphia, I realized what a powerful divide a generation can be.

The Philadelphia that I grew up in was worlds apart from that of Marc Lamont Hill. I grew up in West Philadelphia in the late 1950s and early 1960s. Although the streets of Philadelphia were treacherous then too, my growing up was more shaped by the national turbulence of civil rights and civil disobedience. The gang members that Marc Lamont Hill references in his Preface were my neighbors, friends, and family members. I did not fear them because in many ways I was one of them. The gangs of my growing up settled their disputes with fists, sticks, knives, and, on some rare occasions, sawed-off shotguns. I did not grow up in a time of ubiquitous handguns. My greatest fear was being caught in the "wrong" neighborhood after dark and getting beat up. I did not fear death in the way Marc Lamont Hill's generation (along with this current generation of African American urban youth) do. No, my connection to this text is not about geographical similarities.

What captured my attention (and affection) as I read this book was the fact that its author carefully detailed an innovative research intervention designed to improve educational outcomes for Black and Latino youth. This project begins in the typical "structured for failure" environment so familiar to education researchers. The students are seeking a way to complete diploma requirements. They are assigned to an after-school, early-evening program, and more than a quarter of them fail to show up. In the midst of this no-win situation, Marc Lamont Hill introduces an experimental course entitled, "Hip-Hop Lit" and enlists the help of a somewhat doubtful colleague, "Mr. Columbo."

The notion of using hip-hop as both the content and strategy of urban classrooms is not new. What is new about this text is the careful delineation of how to use this work both for its own intrinsic value and as a kind of scaffolding for access to more conventional genres. For example, Professor Carol D. Lee of Northwestern University has skillfully used students' culture as a model for teaching and learning. In her work, Lee starts with hip-hop lyrics and moves to video representations to help them recognize their own competence in a variety of genres.

Similarly, David Stovall of the University of Illinois at Chicago uses hip-hop culture to help students express their concerns about race and inequality. Also, Jeff Duncan-Andrade of San Francisco State and Ernest Morrell of UCLA both use youth culture, including hip-hop, to help youth to interrogate social problems and develop a civic consciousness.

Marc Lamont Hill distinguishes himself by not merely using hip-hop as a vehicle for study, but by making hip-hop the very object of study. Hill's own connection to hip-hop as a defining strategy for identity development allows him to use hip-hop for exactly what teachers should use literature for—developing the thinking and expanding the worldview of learners.

Good teaching, which I have termed "culturally relevant pedagogy," involves three components—academic achievement (or more specifically, student learning), cultural competence, and socio-political competence. Academic achievement requires that teachers develop a strong focus on student learning. This requires more than covering material. Instead, the teacher must be more concerned with ensuring that students are developing skills and understanding. Cultural competence points to the kinds of tacit knowledge and skills that students must develop to experience success both within their own culture and beyond it. And, socio-political consciousness refers to the ways that students deploy their learning to provide answers for real-world problems.

Marc Lamont Hill's work is a great exemplar of culturally relevant teaching. Rather than choose a group of "popular" rap songs as gimmicks to entice students to be compliant and cooperate in the classroom, Hill searches for enduring and comprehensive themes that define urban life and struggle. Then he looks for music lyrics that address those themes. The work of these lyrics is to help students increase their cultural fluency and to move fluidly across genres and cultural boundaries. Finally, this work helps students make sense of what it means to be a young person of color with limited access to the social benefits of the broader society.

This work is important in the midst of the possibility of educational transition in the 21st century. While the last 8 years have been characterized by one-sided accountability measures (i.e., all sticks and no carrots), many educators are hopeful that a new federal administration will be more receptive to more organic strategies for reaching disenfranchised students and reinvigorating their communities. But even with new federal leadership, what happens at the local level may be impervious to the kind of change and innovation Marc Lamont Hill is referencing here.

Hill is challenging educators to think beyond the narrow constructions of pedagogy that rely on prescriptive and rote strategies. Indeed, this volume is a call for a total transformation of teacher thinking. Instead of attempting to "rescue" students from their communities and cultures, Hill pushes us to see students' cultures as the "stuff" of learning—the curriculum around which to construct classroom-based learning experiences. This approach means that educators will have to learn their students' cultures and communities. This is good news for those of us who see culture as central to learning and especially good news for students who traditionally have been ill-served in the nation's schools.

Hill's book is a beautifully written reminder that the achievement gaps that students (especially Black and Brown students) experience may be more accurately characterized as cultural gaps—between them and their teachers (and the larger society). This is a book that helps us see the power and potential of pedagogy. It is not merely what Hill decides to teach that matters. It is also how he teaches it that connects with the students. The well-meaning, energetic Ivy League graduate who takes on teaching in urban classrooms as a community service project is unlikely to get the kind of training from short-route alternative programs that will help him or her do the type of work Hill describes here. This is work that emanates from full immersion in cultural forms that engage and inspire students.

Some might argue that because they are not African American or Latino they cannot do what Hill did with the students at Howard High, but I would argue that the 2008 U.S. Presidential campaign was an example of two different approaches to the youth vote. The Obama Campaign clearly understood what it took to reach and energize youth. The widespread use of technology—emails, text-messaging, blogs, and videos—is the kind of rapid response that the youth generation demands and the Obama Campaign responded. I reference the campaign not as a partisan but as a response to those who believe that responding to youth culture is merely a palliative for disenfranchised and detached youth. I argue that this kind of response to student needs is a way to mobilize and recruit them into service for the work of the larger society. Such outreach is an epistemological and pedagogical bridge to the future. It honors where students are coming from and propels them to where they need to go. Scholars like Marc Lamont Hill are rare finds in the academy. We will mine this book for the pure ore of community knowledge and cultural passion.

—Gloria Ladson-Billings,
Kellner Family Chair in Urban Education,
University of Wisconsin-Madison

Shout Outs

There's no way that I can pay you back, but my plan is to show you that I understand. You are appreciated.

—Tupac Shakur, "Dear Mama"

Undoubtedly, the most gratifying part of this entire project has been taking the opportunity to thank everyone who has contributed to its completion. While I will inevitably (and inadvertently) omit someone's name, it is my sincerest hope that my love and gratitude will still be felt through these pages.

Without my loving and supportive family, I would not have been able to begin, much less finish this book. From my parents, Leon and Hallean Hill, I have learned the meaning of unconditional love and sacrifice. My brothers, Anthony and Leonard Hill, have taught me to dream dreams bigger than I ever could have dreamed for myself. I'm so proud of you both! My daughter Anya has taught me to question the world with intensity, passion, and sincerity. Thank you for choosing me!!!

A special shout out goes to my squad! James Downs, Matthew Griffin, and R. L'Heureux Lewis have been the best friends and brothers that a person could have. Your humor, support, and generosity have kept me sane and grounded. Cassandra Felix deserves an extra-special shout out for her abiding friendship, endless generosity, and willingness to listen to my ridiculousness on a daily basis. Thank you for everything. Now eat the salsa! Halcyon Francis, Keisha "K. Spraggs" Spraggans, Damon Mitchell, Caitlin Anderson, Rachelle Brunn, Leshawna Coleman, Tracie Curry, Rafiah Davis, Gregg Seaton, Chad Lassiter, Sonia Rosen, Cleo Jacobs, Tyhesha Goss, China Okasi, Audra Price, Kara Jackson, Raphael Freeman, Malik Gore, Royce Smith, Traci English, Cheryl Jones-Walker, Jeanine Staples, Jeannine Amber, Shaun Harper, and Ed Brockenbrough have given far more love and care than I could ever return. I'm so grateful for your friendship. A shout out to "The Block": Natasha Murray, Samantha Murray, and Kimberly

Blagmon. Y'all know what it is! Lalitha Vasudevan has been my consistent partner in writing and random silliness. Melissa Harris-Lacewell has quickly become one of my closest friends and favorite conversation partners. Thank you for being so brilliant, principled, caring, and humble. You are truly the towering intellectual of our generation. (For real!) Let's get our book done! Patrice Berry has offered one of the most loving, selfless, and sincere friendships that I have ever seen. Thank you for being you! Can you stop yelling now?

A special shout out to Meredith Accoo for loving me through the early (and toughest) parts of this book. You were there when I needed someone the most and I will always love you for it. Now tell Meridian, the dopest MC on the planet, to drop that album!

I have been blessed with some of the best mentors and advisors imaginable. From the moment I heard him speak at King Chapel during my freshman year at Morehouse College, Michael Eric Dyson has been an intellectual role model for me. Through his example, I learned that the life of the mind is not only viable but valuable for Black men. Having the privilege to work with him in graduate school was nothing short of a godsend. Mike, your financial, professional, moral, and intellectual support have sustained me under the most hostile conditions. More importantly, you have been a friend and big brother who has stood by me during the toughest times. I love you. Katherine Schultz has been the best advisor, mentor, and advocate that a person could ever have. When I first submitted my graduate school application, you took a big chance on me. Since then, you have respected me enough to take my work seriously and push me beyond what I thought were my limits. I owe more to you than I could ever pay back. I hope to make you proud one day! In Kathleen Hall I found a brilliant anthropologist, caring mentor, and a gentle spirit. Her passion for critical conversations and knack for deep listening continue to support and inspire me. Without the intellectual groundwork of Greg Dimitriadis, this book literally could not have happened. Greg, your tireless work ethic and intellectual adventurousness have been an inspiration to me. Vivian Gadsden has been the mother/mentor that I needed. Thank you for your generosity, wise counsel, and remarkable example. The preface of this book would not exist without the guidance of Susan Lytle, who taught me how not to be afraid to locate myself in and through my work. James Earl Davis has been the best mentor, friend, and brother that I could ask for. Our catching-up sessions remain one of my favorite pastimes! The Africana Studies Program at the University of Pennsylvania provided me a community of support and love more rich than I could have imagined. In particular, I'm grateful to Tukufu Zuberi, Camille Charles, Guthrie Ramsey, and Herman Beavers for their contributions to my growth and development.

Other scholars around the country have been instrumental in my intellectual and personal growth. Mark Anthony Neal and John L. Jackson have shaped my work and professional identity in profound fashion. I look up to you two more than I should probably admit! A shout out goes to all my peoples doing dope work in the field: Salamishah Tillet, Imani Perry, William Jelani Cobb, H. Samy Alim, Maisha Fisher, Korina Jocson, James Braxton Peterson, Boyce Watkins, Valerie Kinloch, and Michael Ralph.

A special shout out goes to my writing group, Emery Petchauer and Lynnette Mawhinney, who have given me great feedback in spite of my triflingness.

My colleagues at Temple University provided me with a wonderful environment in which to think, teach, write, and serve. This would be impossible without the leadership of President Ann Weaver Hart and Dean C. Kent McGuire I could not have asked for better departmental colleagues than Corrine Caldwell, Maia Cucchiara, William Cutler, James Earl Davis, Michael Dorn, Richard Englert, Billie Gastic (*gracias por todo*), Steven Gross, Saul Grossman, Erin Horvat, Vivian Ikpa, Will Jordan, Novella Keith, Michelle Partlow, Joan Shapiro, Kathleen Shaw (I miss you!), and Leonard Waks. A special shout out goes to Marcia Whitaker and Celeste Williams for holding down our department and keeping me sane, organized, and protected. I'm also grateful to my other Temple colleagues, Molefi Asante, Wanda Brooks, James Burns, Jennifer Cromley, Joseph Ducette, Catherine Fiorello, John Francescone, Frank Farley, Judith Goode, Portia Hunt, Jacqueline Leonard, Patricia Louison, Anthony Monteiro, Nathaniel Norment, Aneta Pavlenko, Heidi Ramirez, Michael Smith, and Bryant Simon, for advice, collaboration, and occasional venting sessions.

A special shout out goes to my students: Crystal Barnes, Rebekah Buchanan, Trish Creegan, Sally Gould, H. Bernard Hall, Decoteau Irby, Erin Morales-Williams, Biany Perez, Laura Porterfield, Camika Royal, Kelli Sparrow Mickens, and Ben Starsky. At the risk of sounding corny, I have learned far more from you than I have taught!

A special shout out to Juliet DiLeo Curci and Joshua Bennett for helping me get the manuscript into publishable form. I am extremely grateful to Carole Saltz, Emily Ballengee, and Golnar Nikpour at Teachers College Press. Your vision, critical intelligence, and patience made an anxious first-time author feel comfortable.

In addition to providing me with a research site, the Howard High School community introduced me to a world filled with the most brilliant and beautiful people I have ever encountered. I am particularly indebted to Earl Koger, Samuel Riccobono, Octavia Blount, Bernard Robinson, Robert Pinto, Jesse King, Hiromi Stone-Hernandez, and Michael Picardi for wise counsel, countless laughs, and tireless support of the project.

Most importantly, I am eternally grateful to the students of Howard High School for providing me with the greatest teaching experience of my life. Thank you for sharing your lives with me.

CREDITS

Preface

I was born in 1978 and raised up in Hunting Park, an economically deprived Black neighborhood in North Philadelphia. Because my parents
were teachers, they leveraged their social capital in order to send me to
public elementary and middle schools in The Northeast, the predominately White region of the city. As the only child on my block who left
North Philadelphia to go to school, I was treated and in many ways felt
like an outcast. I did not fit into the White middle-class culture of my
school, as I was neither White nor solidly middle-class. On the other
hand, there were obvious differences between my daily experiences
and those of the people in my own neighborhood. Consequently, I was
never fully comfortable around anyone except the few children that I
met on the school bus who were also transported from their respective
neighborhoods to Northeast Philadelphia.

Although my parents became more successful in their careers and
eventually could afford to move to a middle-class neighborhood,
they remained loyal to the community and decided to stay in North
Philadelphia. Nevertheless, they were concerned about the increasing
amounts of violence in the neighborhood and were reluctant to let me
leave the house to play with other children in the neighborhood. As a
result, I spent much of my free time staring out of the front window,
listening to the sights and sounds of my block, trying to make sense of
the world from which my parents were protecting me.

One day, while sitting in my bedroom, my older brother Anthony
allowed me to listen to one of his favorite rap records, "9mm Goes
Bang" by KRS-One. I cannot remember what my expectations were
before listening, but I am certain that I was totally unprepared for what
I heard. While I fully enjoyed the song on its musical merits, I was both
unsettled and intrigued by the violent story that the song detailed. As I
consumed more of his albums, I developed a very personal connection
to KRS-One and his music. More importantly, I began to reconcile the
stories that KRS was telling with the noises that I was hearing outside

my window. Up to this point, I had heard stories about violence in the neighborhood, but they always seemed distant or surreal. Suddenly, I was able to attach names, faces, and stories to the fuzziest parts of my life. In many ways, hip-hop became my window into a world that was at once familiar and foreign.

After years of resistance, my parents finally relented to the social pressures placed upon them by their middle-class Black friends and moved to Wynnefield, an area of West Philadelphia that was still predominately Black but less economically deprived. Although our family had moved to a "better" neighborhood, they decided to keep me enrolled in school in The Northeast. My parents, who were now relieved to be out of North Philadelphia, finally let me leave the house and interact with other children on a more regular basis.

The acclimation process, however, was quite difficult, as I began to identify more with the White students at the school that I was attending. The more I tried to assimilate into the culture of the school in terms of my speech, dress, and tastes, the less I felt accepted in my own neighborhood. I was having more problems at school than before because regardless of how hard I tried to make them forget, the White students always found ways (sometimes intentionally and at other times unintentionally) to remind me that they were White and I wasn't. Like many children in my circumstance, I felt like I was too White for the Black people and too Black for the White people.

Like many Black youth who wrestle with racial identity issues, I looked for extravagant ways to demonstrate my Blackness. At the same time, hip-hop was developing a new identity as well. Political rappers like Public Enemy, Paris, and Sister Souljah were at the forefront of the hip-hop scene, foregrounding issues of race, class, and politics. Just like when I heard KRS-One for the first time, I felt a connection to political and cultural nationalist rap music that extended beyond a simple appreciation of beats and rhymes. More importantly, the songs provided me with validation, pride, and knowledge that I had otherwise been unable to access.

Because of hip-hop, among other things, I added new layers of racial pride and no longer desired to assimilate into the culture of my White classmates. While I still was not totally accepted by the people in my neighborhood (although my Afrocentric rhetoric and attire did garner some respect and admiration from my peers), I was now more comfortable with my identity as a Black person. I no longer relied on narrow conceptions of Black authenticity, and instead began redefining to link my lessons to my students' personal interests in order to sustain their interest and improve their learning. For my students, most of whom were African American, rap music provided a useful hook that held their interest as I taught them the district-mandated curriculum. This was particularly challenging due to the state's obsession with accountability and standardization, as well as my desire to ensure that my students developed formal academic skills. My decision to pursue graduate study was largely influenced by a desire to determine the efficacy of educational programming that made positive use of students' lived culture while retaining academic rigor, with the ultimate goal of widely influencing classroom practice.

Upon entering graduate school, I began intensive study in anthropology, literacy, cultural studies, and critical pedagogy. While insightful, much of the literature failed to capture the voices of African American youth, even in its discussion of African American youth culture. Furthermore, I found that many of the attempts by non–African American scholars to represent the voices of African American youth by proxy resulted in scholarship that did not represent my experiences or those of my peers, students, and elders. At this point, I made the political and ethical commitment to conduct research that created space for frequently silenced voices to speak to the academic and public communities.

Despite the inadequacy of the current literature with regard to the representation of African American voices and interests, my graduate training pushed my thinking forward and enabled me to develop more sophisticated questions about the relationship among youth, popular culture, identity, and schooling. I was no longer solely concerned with asking "What works?" but also interrogating what it means to "work." Additionally, through the ethnographic gaze I have also begun to ask, "Why does it work?," "For whom does it work?," and "What's at stake when it works?" It is these basic but essential questions that underpin my approach to this book.

In Chapter One I situate the book within several key bodies of scholarly literature, showing how anthropological theory and method produce new questions and valuable insights related to culture, power, and identity.

In Chapter Two I provide a brief description of the context of Hip-Hop Lit. In addition to describing the physical context, I highlight the various structures, processes, and major events that helped to shape my own notions of what it meant to be "really Black." I became more critical of my surroundings, eventually questioning the system that forced me to the Northeast just to get a quality education. Although the mainstream hip-hop community's musical tastes (or at least choices) quickly moved from political to gangster rap and I continued to wrestle with other aspects of my identity, I never relinquished the gifts that hip-hop bestowed upon me.

It is from these experiences that I began to form my intellectual interest in the complex relationships that young people forge with hip-hop culture. In particular, these experiences prompted me to question the ways in which youth use hip-hop texts as complex sites of identity work, enabling them to fashion new notions of self within and outside of formal schooling spaces. Also, my own engagement with hip-hop helped me to consider the ways that youth approach hip-hop texts as sites of public and counterpublic pedagogy that counternarrate their lived experiences.

My motivations for writing this book are largely due to my own experiences as an African American student and teacher within urban classrooms. As a student, I witnessed firsthand how the knowledge, values, and social practices of my community were explicitly or tacitly rejected based on their incompatibility with those of the schools that I attended. Consequently, many of my peers who were active, enthusiastic, and precocious when participating in out-of-school activities were frequently disengaged or disaffected during the regular school day. My desire to understand and improve the conditions that contributed to my friends' estrangement from school led me to shift my major in college from religious studies to education.

As a preservice teacher, I began to take classes within and outside of my major that spoke to the realities of my childhood friends, who also represented the aggregate of urban youth whose lives were not taken seriously within the schoolhouse doors. While theories of indifference, cultural deprivation, and intellectual inferiority were helpful starting points for understanding the problem (as well as the racist ethos of the academy!), they contradicted my own memories of friends who were interested, capable, and encouraged to succeed in school. Convinced that school, and not the students, was the biggest problem, I began to search for ways to link students' in-school and out-of-school lives within my future classroom.

As a Spanish teacher at a school I call "Howard High School," which would eventually serve as the site for my research, I attempted the construction of the Hip-Hop Lit course, as well as the larger schooling and programmatic contexts in which it was situated.

In Chapter Three I detail how notions of "realness" shaped students' negotiation of the course. In particular, I examine how various and often competing constructions of authenticity shaped how students engaged the course texts, negotiated the classroom space, and refashioned various conceptions of identity.

In Chapter Four I illustrate how an engagement with course texts helped to produce a storytelling community in which membership was predicated upon an individual's ability and willingness to share their stories with the rest of the group. These practices helped to produce a variety of classroom identities that created spaces for effective pedagogy, community-building, marginalization, and silencing.

In Chapter Five I detail how students in Hip-Hop Lit used course texts to construct, contest, and reinscribe memories about the past. Through these memories, students were able to reaffirm and challenge particular social identities that informed and reflected their lived experiences. In particular, Hip-Hop Lit students engaged in forms of collective remembering that reiterated and legitimated highly problematic public discourses surrounding the generational identity of today's youth.

In Chapter Six I situate the major themes from the book within the context of classroom practice. Specifically, I outline a tripartite hip-hop pedagogy that takes into consideration the complex identity work that becomes apparent through a multiperspectival analysis of hip-hop–based education contexts. I then discuss the implications of this pedagogy for teachers, educational researchers, and policymakers.

Beats, Rhymes, and Classroom Life

HIP-HOP PEDAGOGY AND
THE POLITICS OF IDENTITY

Given the salience of hip-hop culture in the lives of many urban American youth, the educational community has begun to pay considerable attention to the pedagogical possibilities of hip-hop culture within formal schooling contexts. Drawing from a variety of disciplinary and theoretical traditions, researchers and practitioners have effectively demonstrated the variety of ways that educational contexts are enhanced when hip-hop and other forms of popular culture become a part of the formal school curriculum. In particular, scholars have shown how the elements of hip-hop culture—rap music, turntablism, break dancing, graffiti culture, fashion, and language—can be used within classrooms to improve student motivation, teach critical media literacy, foster critical consciousness, and transmit disciplinary knowledge. These foci and approaches, along with others, collectively comprise the field of study that I refer to as Hip-Hop–Based Education (HHBE).

While current HHBE research has demonstrated the effectiveness of hip-hop–based curricula in contributing to more favorable learning environments and outcomes, insufficient consideration has been given to the cultural stakes attached to such interventions. Ironically, despite the fact that many scholars and practitioners advocate a hip-hop–based curriculum because of its connection to the cultural experiences of students, current scholarship has failed to extend conversations about HHBE beyond the parochial considerations of contemporary educational policy. Instead of carefully unpacking the complex relationships that are forged between youth and hip-hop culture, current classroom research has focused primarily, if not exclusively, on narrow conceptions of educational success such as attendance and standardized test score outcomes. Although these issues are of critical importance, particularly in light of the technocratic demands of No Child Left Behind, they have come at the expense of deeper and broader analyses of the ways that hip-hop–based education shapes and responds to students' lived experiences with hip-hop culture.

This book responds to this gap by showing how student identities are renegotiated when hip-hop culture becomes a part of the official classroom curriculum. Drawing from 18 months of ethnographic fieldwork (1 year of teaching and 6 months of curriculum design) conducted in Hip-Hop Lit, a hip-hop–centered English literature class that I co-taught in an alternative high school, I examine the complex relationships that the students and teachers forged with hip-hop course texts and one another inside and outside of the classroom, as well as how these relationships created a space in which members of the Hip-Hop Lit community performed, contested, and reinscribed a variety of individual and collective identities that informed classroom pedagogy in deeply beneficial and highly challenging ways. Such insights are of critical importance not only for scholars of hip-hop, literacy, teacher education, and youth culture, but also for teachers and policymakers who are concerned with transforming schooling processes in ways that yield more enriching, democratic, and productive outcomes.

Situated within the field of educational anthropology, this book is offered as a rejoinder to the decontextualized, textualist approaches that have pervaded the Educational Left's approach to studying youth and popular culture over the past 2 decades. Such approaches have often prefigured the relationship between youth and popular culture, resulting in romantic accounts of youth resistance or pessimistic narratives of domination. From this posture, we fail to fully comprehend the complex and often unpredictable ways that youth engage hip-hop and other popular culture texts within and outside of formal schooling contexts. Additionally, such approaches provide inadequate access to the relationships between youth and increasingly influential processes such as neoliberal globalization, transnational cultural flows, and the expanding role of popular culture in the construction of racial, (trans)national, and generational identities (e.g., Appadurai, 1991; Dolby & Rizvi, 2007; Ginsburg, Abu-Lughod, & Larkin, 2002; Jackson, 2005; Thomas, 2004).

As an applied ethnographic project, this study explicitly aims to link its insights to practical concerns related to classroom pedagogy. This approach is animated by the current failure of educational researchers to effect tangible shifts in educational policy and practice. This is not to suggest that our intellectual labor be reduced to the shortsighted visions of those researchers, policymakers, and practitioners who fetishize randomized experimentation, quantifiable outcomes, and standardized classroom procedures. Indeed, none of these are prominent themes within the book. Rather, it is my contention that any politically and ethically credible research agenda must appeal to more than the hedonistic proclivities of those academics who, like myself, find personal pleasure in the indulgence of theory for theory's sake. As the quotes from Stuart Hall and De La Soul that begin this chapter suggest, the cultural, political, and economic exigencies of the day are far too urgent—the stakes too high—for such decadence. Thus, it is the primary goal of this book to connect theory, research, and classroom practice by linking ethnographic inquiry to engaged praxis.

By outlining several key bodies of literature that shape HHBE, I hope to elucidate how anthropological theory and method can enrich current discussions by spotlighting issues of identity, power, and local meaning.

HIP-HOP STUDIES

For more than a decade, hip-hop culture has been the object of critical analysis within the academy. Given the growing public anxiety about the rise of gangster rap in the early 1990s, much of the early scholarship on hip-hop emerged in response to alleged links between rap music and social pathology. In the social sciences, this reactionary stance resulted in a series of studies by psychologists and other behaviorists who attempted to test the effects of rap music consumption on youth self-esteem, violence, and hypersexuality (Hall, 1998; Johnson et al., 1995; Took & Weiss, 1994; Tyson, 2002). Although this research provided critical and nuanced rejoinders to the moral panic of the day, the narrow focus of the studies ignored issues of culture, identity, and power with regard to youth engagement with hip-hop. As a result, scholars gained considerable insight into the extent to which hip-hop "does" things to young people, yet very little was learned about the motivations, processes, or nonclinical consequences of youth engagement with hip-hop.

In the humanities, hip-hop scholars have relied upon close readings of hip-hop texts, particularly rap music and videos, to show how they reflect and inform particular formations of gender (e.g., hooks, 1994; Pough, 2004; Sharpley-Whiting, 2007), race (e.g., Dyson, 1993, 2007; Forman, 2002), and political economy (e.g., Kelley, 1998; McLaren, 1999; Quinn, 2005). Through these readings, hip-hop studies scholars have demonstrated the complexities, contradictions, and redemptive dimensions of hip-hop culture. Although these textual analyses have provided considerable insight into the structures and forces that mediate hip-hop cultural production, they are largely inadequate for making sense of the ways that youth approach, interpret, and respond to hip-hop texts within their daily lives. Such insights, which are illuminated through ethnographic research, are critical for tracking the ways that youth complicate and often defy *a priori* understandings of the relationships between youth and hip-hop culture.

The need for anthropological perspectives on youth engagement with hip-hop culture is further substantiated by the small but growing body of ethnographic fieldwork. Condry (2007) shows how global cultural flows allow youth in Japan to appropriate and refashion American hip-hop in order to construct identities as "Yellow B-Boys." Linguistic anthropologists such as Alim (2006) and Cutler (2001) detail the complex ways that youth deploy "Hip Hop Nation Language" in order to construct racialized identities that link them to literal and imagined communities that traverse local and national boundaries. While Alim focuses on the language practices of African American youth who consume and produce hip-hop culture, Cutler's study shows how White middle-class youth deploy hip-hop discourse in order to construct themselves as authentic members of an imagined hip-hop community that privileges "urban Black street experiences" (p. 211). Dimitriadis (2001), whose ethnographic study was conducted in a Midwestern United States community center, demonstrates how students used popular hip-hop texts in order to construct notions of history, self, and community.

Although these studies (with the exception of Dimitriadis) do not explicitly address issues of schooling, they nonetheless expose the complex and often unpredictable ways that youth use hip-hop culture in order to fashion the very selves that enter and navigate educational contexts. This book follows these studies by examining how youth use hip-hop texts to negotiate particular conceptions of self and the social world, both of which affect how they negotiate the Hip-Hop Lit classroom. Such insights are necessary for understanding the cultural dynamics of HHBE contexts, as well as schooling contexts more broadly.

HIP-HOP AS CRITICAL PEDAGOGY

Academic investigation into the use of hip-hop in the classroom has been largely undergirded by theory that lies at the intersection of the critical pedagogy and cultural studies traditions. While early work in the field of critical pedagogy focused on the role of modern schools in reproducing the relations of capitalism (e.g., Bernstein, 1977; Bowles & Gintis, 1976; Jackson, 1968), the turn to cultural studies resulted in an increased focus on the relationship between everyday cultural practices and the politics of schooling. In particular, critical pedagogues have examined the ways in which formal schooling contexts not only operate as sites for transmitting disciplinary knowledge, but also as spaces within which particular formations of knowledge are constructed and legitimated (Giroux, 1994). Moving beyond the cultural elitism of bourgeois humanist (e.g., Arnold, 1932) and Marxist traditions (e.g, Adorno & Horkheimer, 1944), critical pedagogy scholars have also followed cultural studies theorists in rejecting arbitrary distinctions between "high" and "low" culture. In doing so, they have created theoretical room for examining the complex ways that popular culture operates as a rich and valuable site for public pedagogy within and, more significantly, outside of school.

In addition to challenging Frankfurt School approaches to popular culture, critical pedagogy and cultural studies scholars have also acknowledged and resisted the romantic interpretations of "cultural populists" (McGuigan, 1992) who have focused on the primacy of pleasure and resistance in popular culture consumption. The cultural populist approach, perhaps best exemplified by the work of John Fiske (1979, 1987, 1989), has demonstrated how individuals consume popular culture in ways that challenge early Frankfurt School notions of pure domination. Informed by postmodern notions of hybridity, local meaning, and the reduced salience of authorial intentionality, cultural populists have also demonstrated the "fallacy of internalism" (Thompson, 1990), or the belief that textual analysis is a sufficient method for determining the relationship between individuals and popular culture texts. While useful for keeping track of individual agency and resistance, such approaches have simultaneously overestimated the ability of individuals to recognize and ward off dominant ideologies, and underestimated the capacity of broader institutions (media, the state, etc.) to produce taste, desire, and choice (Morley, 1992; Murdock, 1997).

Critical pedagogues have created space for examining popular culture as a complex and contested site for both resistance and domination. Furthermore, they have buttressed the need for what Kellner (1992) refers to as a "multiperspectival" approach to cultural studies that negotiates the relationships between text, context, and reception. This approach is comprised of three parts: 1) political culture (text production, formula, and convention); 2) textual analysis (analyzing discourse/narrative structure, understanding ideological positions, image construction, and effects); and 3) audience reception (How do people actually read these cultural texts? How do these texts affect everyday life?) (Freedman, 2003, p. 246). Multiperspectival analysis is an essential component of critical pedagogy's engagement with popular culture, as it helps to identify and undermine the pervasiveness of dominant perspectives while simultaneously tracking the ways that these perspectives are reproduced and resisted.

Despite a clear theoretical commitment to the cultural studies tradition, critical pedagogy scholars have largely ignored multiperspectival analyses in favor of rigid textual approaches. As a consequence, rich ethnographic investigations into the relationships between youth and popular culture have been subordinated to rigid textual analyses of popular music, television, and film (Daspit & Weaver, 2001; Dimitriadis, 2001; Hill & Vasudevan, 2008). For example, Farber and Holm (1994), in their critical reading of the popular school films *Lean on Me*, *Dead Poets Society*, and *Stand and Deliver*, discuss how the portrayal of the American educator as hero (particularly *Lean on Me*'s Joe Clark and *Stand and Deliver*'s Jaime Escalante) hide the larger structural problems of public schools. Giroux and McLaren (1989) argue that the authoritarian, militaristic leadership style of Joe Clark reflected the Reagan administration's view that the solution to ghetto schooling problems was to "get tough" (p. xix). Giroux (1996) and Kellner (1995), in their readings of *Slackers*, see the film as yet another depressing depiction of postmodern youth. Although Giroux does acknowledge that his students made alternate readings of the film, Daspit and Weaver (2001) point out that this is done only "as a side-bar rather than an alternative narrative flowing along side of Giroux's own reading" (p. xvii).

These critical textual analyses are indispensable for spotlighting the overt and latent ideological structures within popular texts, as well as the pedagogical role that popular culture texts play in the lives of youth. Nevertheless, a nearly exclusive focus on ideological critique obscures the unique, complex, and often unpredictable connections that individuals forge with popular culture texts (Dimitriadis, 2001; Hill & Vasudevan, 2008). For example, in her qualitative study of African American middle school teachers' readings of *Lean on Me*, Smith (2000) found that there existed more than the two readings that she had considered, which were the ones offered by Giroux and McLaren and the "one that power brokers intended" (p. 22). Instead she found that African American teachers viewed the presence of Joe Clark, an African American, as a welcome divergence from previous schooling films, where the savior was presented in the personage of "a crusading European American interloper" (p. 22). While these interpretations do not negate critical pedagogues' analyses, they provide a level of emic texture and nuance that thickens our understanding of the relationship between individuals and popular texts. Similarly, students often make sense of hip-hop texts in ways that render prefigured analyses inadequate or inaccurate. Again, while these meaning-making processes are not divorced from the dominant discourses that are spotlighted through close textual analysis, they can only be fully understood through multiperspectival ethnographic analyses that consider both structure and agency, text and context. Such work is requisite for advancing theory, as well as constructing culturally responsive curriculum and pedagogy.

INTERROGATING CULTURAL RELEVANCE

While critical pedagogy has strongly influenced HHBE theory, the field of culturally relevant pedagogy has largely informed its classroom application. Since the early 1990s, scholars of culturally relevant pedagogy have demonstrated the importance of appealing to the experiences, cultural orientations, values, and worldviews of students in order to effectuate greater educational outcomes. Of particular significance is the work of Carol Lee (1993, 1995a, 1995b), whose Cultural Modeling framework advocates the design of "instruction that makes explicit connections between students' everyday knowledge and the demands of subject-matter learning" (Lee, Spencer, & Harpalani, 2003, p. 7). Using this framework, Lee investigated the effectiveness of "signifying," a central trope of African diasporic culture, as a scaffold for teaching and learning literary interpretation. Drawing on prior research that asserted that African American students tend to perform better in small, cooperative learning groups (Boykin, 1986; Slavin, 1990; Slavin & Oickle, 1981), Lee's experimental group received small-group instruction and utilized culturally relevant vernacular texts as the primary literary source by which to teach literary interpretive skills. In Lee's study, the experimental group showed statistically significant gains in literal and inferential reading categories. In addition to Lee's quantitative work, many qualitative studies (e.g., Gay, 2000; Howard, 2001; Ladson-Billings, 1994, 1998; Leonard & Hill, 2008) have demonstrated how culturally relevant classroom interventions positively contribute to student confidence, curricular engagement, and teacher–student relationships.

Although the current body of literature substantiates the effectiveness of culturally relevant curriculum and pedagogy with regard to the above-mentioned factors, there remains a dearth of scholarship examining issues of power and position. Specifically, scholars have yet to thoroughly interrogate how the reorganization of official classroom knowledge, expertise, and culture affects the ways in which students and teachers negotiate the classroom context. While many studies have appropriately detailed how the relocation of particular cultural formations from the margins to the center of the curriculum has engendered feelings of empowerment and possibility among students, there has been little discussion of how such processes simultaneously marginalize other members of the classroom community. Consequently, scholars inevitably underwrite static and essentialized conceptions of culture by assuming that all students share a common set of experiences and subjectivities that can be appealed to through a singular set of curricular and pedagogical choices. Such a move also underwrites new forms of cultural hegemony by ignoring individuals who fall outside the boundaries of the newly centered culture. For example, by constructing an African-centered curriculum for all "Black" students, scholars reinforce a universal conception of "Blackness" that ignores the complex subjectivities that are constituted by the political, cultural, and economic processes that animate racial formation (Dolby, 2001; Jackson, 2005; Omi & Winant, 1994). Also, by ignoring the effects of an African-centered curriculum intervention on non-Black students, scholars and practitioners undermine the humanistic notion of "pluralism without hierarchy" (Asante, 1991, p. 271) upon which African-centered pedagogy rests.

The failure to critically interrogate marginalized cultures also reflects a tendency among social scientists to "sanitize the internal politics of the dominated" (Ortner, 2006, p. 47) by ignoring or understating the extent to which marginalized cultures contain practices that warrant critique. Within anthropology, this tendency has resulted in studies that highlight external domination and romanticize subaltern resistance without critiquing internal contradictions, particularly along lines of gender (Abu-Lughod, 1990; Lukose, 2007; Ortner, 2006). With regard to educational research, this approach has allowed us to ignore the ways in which cultural relevance, particularly for students of color, can signify not only emancipatory but socially reproductive possibilities. Furthermore, this approach has resulted in highly celebratory studies that demonstrate the virtues and successes of culturally based interventions without acknowledging potential dilemmas, tensions, contradictions, and constraints.

With regard to classroom practice, a nearly exclusive focus on these "victory narratives" (Lather, 1993) implicitly forecasts an unproblematic classroom pedagogy devoid of silencing, marginalization, and domination. Throughout this book, however, I demonstrate that the use of culturally relevant (in this case, hip-hop–based) pedagogies inevitably creates spaces of both voice and silence, centering and marginalization, empowerment and domination. Within Hip-Hop Lit, the students engaged hip-hop texts and one another in ways that enabled critical conversations and transgressive moments. Through the Hip-Hop classroom, and particularly through hip-hop texts, students were able to craft new spaces and ways to offer their voices. Within the same context, and sometimes at the very same moments, students revealed highly problematic ideologies that were in direct conversation with, and sometimes buttressed by, prominent themes within mainstream hip-hop culture. It is within this complex and often contradictory space that I examine the relationships between hip-hop culture, pedagogy, and youth identities.

HIP-HOP–BASED EDUCATION AND THE POLITICS OF IDENTITY

For more than a decade, a growing body of scholarship has focused on the intersections among hip-hop culture, youth, and pedagogy. This literature, which I refer to as Hip-Hop–Based Education (HHBE), has drawn on a variety of theoretical, empirical, and practical insights in order to substantiate the importance and effectiveness of linking various aspects of hip-hop culture to formal and informal educational processes. In particular, HHBE scholars have persuasively shown how hip-hop–based curricular interventions can help to scaffold canonical knowledge (Hill, 2008; Morrell & Duncan-Andrade, 2002; Rice, 2003), increase student engagement (Mahiri, 1998; Stovall, 2006), and raise critical consciousness (Dimitriadis, 2001; Duncan-Andrade & Morrell, 2005; Hill, 2006; Pardue, 2004). Through this growing body of research, HHBE scholars have constructed a strong case for the pedagogical value of HHBE across a variety of contexts.

For anthropologists of education, however, the insights garnered from the current body of scholarship must be accompanied by broader considerations of culture and identity within HHBE contexts. While several HHBE scholars (e.g., Hill, 2006; Morrell & Duncan-Andrade, 2002) have initiated this conversation by demonstrating how HHBE classrooms enable the articulation of student voice and the reconsideration of school-sanctioned knowledge, these issues have been largely secondary to spotlighting the utility of hip-hop texts for scaffolding traditional knowledge, motivating students, and developing critical media literacy. While useful, such foci do not facilitate a thorough examination of HHBE with respect to the reconstitution of classroom power relations, pedagogy, and identities. As Pennycook (2005) argues, a careful interrogation of these relationships requires HHBE scholars to move beyond a focus on the validation of hip-hop and other forms of popular culture within the classroom:

> A model of validation of popular culture has a number of limitations, based as it is primarily on a functional account of how the inclusion of popular culture in education may enhance literacy skills and allow for greater and more varied student voice. This overlooks the central role of popular culture in identity formation, the fluidity and location of engagement in popular culture, and the need for pedagogies to engage rather than include. (p. 30)

While the current body of HHBE literature has effectively demonstrated the need for and efficacy of pedagogies of inclusion, there is a considerable lack of ethnographic research that interrogates the relationship between hip-hop and identity formation, as well as the "fluidity and location of engagement" in hip-hop culture. Such insights are critical for forging deeper and more authentically responsive classroom pedagogies.

Although much of the work in Hip-Hop Studies provides considerable insight into the relationships between hip-hop culture and youth identity formation, there remains a need to examine these issues in light of the formal schooling context. Through his study of Somalian immigrants in North American high schools, Forman (2005) shows how the high school context serves as a site for earning citizenship within an imagined Hip-Hop Nation. By appropriating the aesthetic, linguistic, and consumption practices of American hip-hop culture, Somalian teenagers were able to develop a sense of "Blackness" that enabled valuable social connections within the school. Ibrahim (1999) provides one of the few studies that directly articulate youth identity work to considerations of teaching and learning. For the students in his English as a Second Language course, all of whom were French-speaking continental African immigrants, hip-hop culture provided a site for learning "Black stylized English" and constructing Black American identities that informed "what and how they linguistically and cul-turally learn[ed]" (p. 349). While the current research underscores the need for more studies that examine how youth identity work informs classroom pedagogy, there also remains a need for ethnographic field-work that views the classroom context as a unique site for contesting, reflecting, or constituting particular identities. This book contributes to these gaps by considering the ways in which Hip-Hop Lit course texts, as well as the Hip-Hop Lit classroom itself, operated as a site for complex negotiations of student identity. Through this hip-hop–centered context, students were able to "try on" (Weis & Fine, 2000) new conceptions of self, some highly productive and ennobling and others deeply contradictory and problematic, that shaped how they understood themselves, the classroom, school, and the broader social world.

2

"Spaces and Places We Fly"

The Texts and Contexts of Hip-Hop Lit

"Text without context is pretext"
                                    —Rev. Jesse L. Jackson Sr.

"Where I'm from, it be like 'run your coat, Black'
Jupiter, keeps her fat beats by the pack
Where I'm from, nappy hair is life
We be readin' Marx where I'm from
The kids be rockin' Clarks where I'm from
You turn around your cap, you talk over a beat
and dig some sounds boomin' out a jeep"
                        —Digable Planets, "Where I'm From"

In many ways, Howard High School (HHS) is like countless urban schools around the United States. A small comprehensive high school located in South Philadelphia, HHS has a student population of 1,200 with a 72% attendance rate. Like the neighborhood itself, HHS is racially diverse (41.5% Black, 26.8% Asian American, 24.4% White, and 6.9% Latino) but predominately Black. Most of the students in the school qualify for free or reduced-price lunch, a standard measure of student poverty levels. Originally a junior high school, HHS is quite small in comparison to most city high schools and attracts students from all over the city who want an alternative to the larger neighborhood high schools but are unable to meet the entrance requirements of the city's magnet schools. Despite the school's citywide appeal, the majority of families in the immediate vicinity, most of whom are White, send their children to area parochial schools.

HHS is divided into four small learning communities: Venturing Into Professions, which prepares students for service industry jobs after graduation; Multicultural, which focuses on computer science and technology; Urban Education, which prepares students for potential

careers as teachers; and Law Academy, the most academically rigorous program, designed for students interested in careers as lawyers.
Despite the majority status of African American and Latino students
at HHS, few are enrolled in Law Academy. Most minority students are
placed, irrespective of academic interest or performance, into Venturing Into Professions, which has a college acceptance rate of less than
40%, including community college.

Like most urban schools, HHS is under pressure from the school
district to improve its overall academic performance in compliance
with the No Child Left Behind Act. In 2001–02, the most recent year
for which the school would provide standardized test scores, 84.1%
of students performed below basic levels in math, 72.8% scored below
basic levels in reading, and 75.7% scored below basic levels in science
(School District of Philadelphia, 2003). In response to this pressure,
HHS administrators (all of whom, like their predecessors, have been
at the school for less than 2 years) initiated a schoolwide campaign to
"get tough" on teachers and students, both of whom are considered to
be part of the school's academic problems. Consequently, the school
has witnessed a dramatic increase in teacher and student transfers,
suspensions, and other punitive disciplinary actions.

In-school and out-of-school violence is one of the primary concerns
of teachers and administrators at HHS. In addition to the random
fights that are typical in many high schools, HHS is a primary site for
intra-neighborhood violence. For more than 50 years, South Philadelphia has contained feuds between various street gangs that are organized around four "blocks": 5th Street, 7th Street, 12th Street, and 24th
Street. Students (particularly African American and Latino males) who
live in between these streets typically align themselves with the closest
corresponding street—for example, a student who lived on 9th Street
would likely associate with the 7th Street gang, and when asked where
he was from, he would likely reply that he was from 7th Street. Gang
violence reached its peak in the summer of 2002, when three students
from 5th Street were shot and killed by adults from another block.
When school reopened in September, student assaults were so common that the school transferred large numbers of students from 12th
and 24th Street to other schools for their own safety.

Although HHS is a relatively neutral site, it nonetheless poses a dangerous problem for students who live farthest away from the school,
as they must pass through multiple neighborhoods to return home.
As a consequence of this situation, students from these neighborhoods

typically travel in groups of four or more to protect themselves and elect to stay home rather than go to school alone. Others have elected to transfer to schools outside the neighborhood or attend the Twilight Program to avoid violence.

It is against the tragically familiar backdrop of HHS that I provide a descriptive analysis of the Hip-Hop Lit context. In particular, this chapter provides a detailed description of the Hip-Hop Lit classroom, as well as the broader programs, structures, processes, and events that contributed to its development. Through this description, I aim to highlight Hip-Hop Lit's distinctive features, as well as the ways that it mirrors countless urban settings around the nation. Such an analysis not only lends descriptive texture to this ethnographic narrative, but also spotlights the study's applicability beyond its particular contextual boundaries.

THE TWILIGHT PROGRAM

The Howard High School Twilight Program, known by most simply as "Twilight," is an evening education program funded by the School District of Philadelphia. Although the program was initially designed for students over the age of 18 to return to school and complete the requirements for a high school diploma, Twilight has become a catchall for students who do not fit comfortably within the day school environment. Teen parents, day school "behavior problems," students whose financial burdens forced them to work during the day, students with excessive lateness, and those seeking refuge from school violence are the primary populations who enroll in the program. Students in the program range in age from 15 to 23, with the average student in the program being 17 years old. The program offers opportunities for students to complete their high school education by obtaining credits in Spanish, English, math, science, and social studies, as well as a range of elective courses.

The Twilight school day officially begins at 3:15 P.M. and ends at 6:15 P.M., although student lateness and teacher fatigue have made the de facto hours of operation 3:30 to 6:00. The school year is divided into two 4-month semesters with a 3-week break in January. Each school day is divided into two 90-minute periods, with a 30-minute de facto break that is created by first-period teachers who end class fifteen minutes early and second-period teachers who begin fifteen minutes late.

Although students are required to attend from Monday to Thursday, the average daily attendance rate is less than 50%. A large reason for this is the high number of truant students who only remain on the official attendance rolls in order to satisfy the terms of their parole agreements. Nevertheless, most teachers and administrators do not expect students to attend daily and rarely enforce the school's attendance policy.

Unlike day school, the Twilight Program faces little administrative or governmental pressure with regard to student performance. Although students are required to take the state standardized tests, the Twilight Program is generally granted a great deal of curricular flexibility. As Mr. Ormond, the program director, explained, "They make us give the kids tests just to protect themselves but they're happy if we can just keep them safe and out of trouble and graduate a few of them." While the lack of attention given to Twilight students creates difficulty in obtaining material and human resources, it also affords Mr. Ormond with a great deal of curricular flexibility. He explains:

> Sometimes I think they forget we're up here. It's bad in a way
> because you can't always get what you need. It's good, though,
> because students are serviced better without all of the bureau-
> cracy. For example, in Twilight I have to offer English and math
> but other than that I can pretty much do what I want. Last year
> I let Smith [a former teacher in the program] teach a film class.
> Try doing that in day school!

The degree of freedom to which Mr. Ormond alludes is the primary reason for my decision to conduct the Hip-Hop Lit project within the Twilight Program as opposed to traditional day school.

CONSTRUCTING HIP-HOP LIT

The Hip-Hop Lit project began as part of an assignment for a graduate school urban education seminar. For the project, a preservice teacher and I brought in rap songs once a week and had students engage in various forms of interpretation and discussion. The success of the project prompted me to propose a yearlong English elective course at Howard High School, where I had previously taught for 2 years. Later that year, I approached Mr. Ormond about conducting a full-fledged yearlong study within the Twilight Program. Although he quickly agreed to support the project, he reminded me that union regulations stated that I could not legally teach a school district course without applying for a job and competing against other applicants. Mr. Ormond requested that I co-teach the course with an English teacher who would serve as the official instructor in order to please the administration and satisfy legal requirements.

FINDING A PARTNER

After receiving conditional approval from Mr. Ormond, I immediately contacted Mr. Smith, a close friend and former colleague, about co-teaching Hip-Hop Lit with me. Mr. Smith was an extremely talented and popular teacher with a great deal of classroom experience as well as an expressed interest in bridging popular culture and English education. He became interested in the Hip-Hop Lit project the previous year, when I used his classroom to conduct my graduate course project. Mr. Smith immediately agreed to co-teach the course, and we planned to meet over the summer to discuss details. In April, however, Mr. Smith notified me that he had been promoted to assistant principal at a nearby school and would be leaving HHS at the end of the summer. He suggested that I contact Mr. Jones, another experienced English teacher who was interested in the project. Mr. Jones quickly agreed to work with me, but warned that he might be granted the transfer that he had recently requested to one of the city's magnet schools. Less than 2 weeks later, Mr. Jones contacted me and informed me that he would not be returning to HHS for the upcoming school year.

At this point I turned to Mr. Colombo, another former colleague who was teaching in the Twilight Program. Despite his lack of familiarity with hip-hop, he brought an interesting background that contrasted with mine. Mr. Colombo was a 30-year-old White classroom teacher with 4 years of English teaching experience. Although he had little knowledge and interest in hip-hop culture, he expressed an interest in "learning more about what the students are into." I was a 24-year-old African American doctoral student and a former Spanish teacher at HHS, where I still taught summer school. Unlike Mr. Colombo, I was an active participant in the hip-hop community as a critic, journalist, scholar, and lifelong listener.

I had considered working with Mr. Colombo at the beginning but decided not to because of the general perception around the school that he was not an effective classroom teacher. I was reminded of this sentiment when I mentioned to a group of teachers that I would be co-teaching with Mr. Colombo. After a full minute of laughter, one of them added, "Good luck, Hill. You have *no* idea what you're getting into." I would soon find out that, as I had frequently found to be the case in urban schools, their concerns about his effectiveness as a teacher were based on his classroom management skills. Although he was by his own admission "struggling" in that area, I considered classroom management to be one of my strengths and decided that a partnership would be beneficial to both of us. More practically, I was eager to begin the project and felt like I had few viable alternatives. We decided to begin meeting twice a week in May in order to construct the basic framework for the course, which would begin in September.

DESIGNING AND TEACHING HIP-HOP LIT

In preparation for constructing and teaching the Hip-Hop Lit curriculum, I began to develop a theoretical framework for the course. Through the framework, which I called *hip-hop literacy*, I wanted the course to enable students to develop "the ability to read and write in a manner that allows one to de-center dominant (hegemonic) conceptions of reality and relocate the specific experiences, values, and codes of the hip-hop community from the periphery to the center" (Hill, 2008, p. 263). Also, drawing from critical race theory's focus on counter-storytelling as a means by which to move the experiences of marginalized people to the center of public discourse (Delgado Bernal, 2002; Guinier & Torres, 2002; Ladson-Billings, 1998), I wanted Hip-Hop Lit to allow the experiences of the students and the authors to be the centerpiece of the course. With this goal in mind, I began my deliberations with Mr. Colombo.

For our first meeting, I asked Mr. Colombo to bring a broad list of curricular objectives that he thought were important. We planned to compare our lists, resolve any contradictions, and begin planning the course based on the emergent goals. When we met, we read each other's prepared list:

> *Marc's goals*: 1) Develop a course that allows us to easily keep track of students' interpretations of the popular; 2) Students will be able to employ traditional literary interpretive

strategies; 3) Create an environment conducive to hip-hop literacy; 4) Use hip-hop pedagogical strategies with respect to reader/text, teacher/student, and curriculum/instruction.

Colombo's goals: 1) Students will be able to create three types of essays: persuasive, narrative, and informational; 2) Students will be able to discuss, analyze, construct, and interpret old and modern poetry; 3) Students will be able to employ literary interpretive skills.

We decided that our lists were not only reconcilable but reflective of a fairly similar vision for the class. By the end of the second meeting, we officially named the course (based on Mr. Colombo's suggestion) "Hip-Hop Lit" and described it as following on the course syllabus:

This course will examine various elements of literary inter-pretation and criticism through the lens of hip-hop culture. Students will encounter, learn, and demonstrate traditional and nontraditional methods of literary analysis and critique using hip-hop texts as the primary sources.

From this point, we divided the course into thematic units in order to better focus our selection of texts. We decided on the following six themes: Roots of Hip-Hop and Literature, Love, Family, "The Hood," Politics, and Despair. Each unit was to contain a minimum of eight texts, four or five that were selected by Mr. Colombo and me, and three or four that were selected by individual students and subject to our approval.

Course Texts

Although Mr. Colombo and I initially decided that we would each select course texts, he soon informed me that he was uncomfortable participating in the process because of his lack of familiarity with rap music and hip-hop culture. We agreed that I would choose the course texts and he would spend time reading the selections that I made and listening to the CD that I would prepare for him.

The first decision that I made when selecting course texts was that I would refrain from using well-known (i.e., Top 40) songs as potential choices. I made this choice for several reasons: I wanted to expose the students to a wider range of hip-hop artists and texts; it was extremely difficult to find Top 40 songs that substantively dealt with the themes that Mr. Colombo and I had chosen; also, I was concerned that the students had already committed the songs to memory, making it more difficult for them to approach them as literature worthy of close reading as opposed to rote recitation.

After deciding on the types of songs that I wanted to include in the course, I began to compile texts. I searched through the largest and most accurate hip-hop lyric archives available—the most useful being the Original Hip-Hop Lyrics Archive (www.ohhla.com)—in search of songs that matched the six course themes. I began my search by looking for artists whose work I associated with each theme. For example, I began looking for "Love" songs by searching the work of Lauryn Hill; I started my search for "Hood" songs by examining Nas's work. I also contacted more than 50 friends and colleagues within the field of education, music, and journalism, requesting suggestions for appropriate songs.

After compiling more than 200 songs, I began to look for songs that, based on their form and content, were appropriate for the course. With regard to form, I was interested in texts whose structure allowed for close and engaged reading as printed text. Although I accepted the fact that many of the texts would contain profanity or depict violence, I was extremely reluctant to use texts that contained gratuitous amounts of either. Also, I immediately eliminated texts that I found to be primarily racist, misogynist, or homophobic and heterosexist. Although I saw the class as a space to examine and challenge these discourses, I worried that reading potentially offensive texts would worry the administration and shift the class's primary focus from literary interpretation to critical media literacy. For this reason, I eliminated several potentially provocative and useful pieces based on their content. For example, I decided to exclude Eminem's "If I Had" from the "Despair" unit based on its explicit language and Eminem's larger corpus of homophobic, sexist, and as recently revealed racist work (Hill, 2008). Also, I was initially interested in using Tupac's "Me and My Girlfriend" because of its powerful use of metaphor but eventually removed it from the list because of its excessive violence and profanity, as well its objectification of women—the "girlfriend" in the song was a metaphor for his handgun. Conversely, I included several songs by Nas, Jay-Z, and Common, whose bodies of work are littered with sexist and homophobic lyrics, because of their individual literary value and potential for critical interrogation.

1

"Stakes Is High"

Toward an Anthropology
of Hip-Hop–Based Education

"Against the urgency of people dying in the streets, what in God's name is the point of cultural studies? What is the point of the study of representations, if there is no response to the question of what you say to someone who wants to know if they should take a drug and if that means they'll die two days later or a few months earlier? At that point, I think anybody who is into cultural studies seriously as an intellectual practice, must feel, on their pulse, its ephemerality, its insubstantiality, how little it registers, how little we've been able to change anything or get anybody to do anything. If you don't feel that as one tension in the work that you are doing, theory has let you off the hook."
     —Stuart Hall, "Cultural Studies and Its Theoretical Legacies"

"Stakes Is High"

     —De La Soul

Since its birth on the streets of New York in the 1970s, hip-hop culture has been transformed from a local youth movement to an international phenomenon. From the iPods of suburban American teens to revolutionary movements in the Global South, the sites, sounds, and spectacles of hip-hop have become a central feature of an increasingly globalized cultural landscape. Despite its roots within U.S., Caribbean, and African diasporic traditions, hip-hop has been consumed and refashioned in ways that respond to the experiences, traditions, imaginations, and desires of young people throughout the world. Such developments speak to the significance of hip-hop not only as a popular culture text, but also as a rich site for complex forms of identity work.

Figure 2.1. Basic Course Texts

Roots of Hip-Hop & Literature	Love	Family	The Hood	Politics	Despair
"The Message" by Grandmaster Flash and the Furious Five	"Manifest" (Third Verse) by Fugees	"Ms. Jackson" by Outkast	"Project Window" by Nas	"I Can" by Nas	"Suicidal Thoughts" by Notorious B.I.G.
"I Used to Love H.E.R." by Common	"Between Me You and Liberation" by Common	"Dear Mama" by Tupac	"Ballad for a Fallen Soldier" by Jay-Z	"The Experience" by Goodie M.O.B.	"Dynasty Intro" by Jay-Z
"Love of My Life" by Erykah Badu and Common	"Ms. Fat Booty" by Mos Def	"Where Have You Been" by Jay-Z and Beanie Sigel	"Summertime" by DJ Jazzy Jeff and the Fresh Prince	"I Wanna Talk to You" By Nas	"I Refuse Limitations" by Goodie M.O.B.
"Rapper's Delight" by Sugar Hill Gang	"The Light" by Common	"Retrospect for Life" by Common	"Things Done Changed" by Notorious B.I.G.	"Fuck tha Police" by N.W.A.	"Tennessee" by Arrested Development
	"Love Is Blind" by Eve	"La Femme Fatal" by Digable Planets	"Year of the Dragon" by Wyclef & Lauryn Hill	"They Schools" by dead prez	

After several weeks of compiling and deliberating, I eventually decided on the texts shown in Figure 2.1.

The Curriculum

In constructing the curriculum, Mr. Colombo and I agreed that we wanted the course to focus on hip-hop texts as literature and not merely the printed versions of music. For this reason we decided not to include music as a part of the curriculum. Also, in an effort to focus the students on the literary value of the readings, we consistently referred to the artists as "authors" and the songs as "texts."

At our first meeting, Mr. Colombo and I decided that after selecting the course texts we would analyze the selections closely in order to highlight the particular literary strategies that were deployed by each author. After giving Mr. Colombo the list of texts, he sent me the following e-mail:

Marc,

I think you're doing a great job with the class so far. Since you picked the songs I think it'd be easier if you made up the syllabus and I just check it to see if I'm cool with everything. That way we can be consistent and make sure everything is how you like it.

Although I was becoming increasingly frustrated with Mr. Colombo's lack of involvement with the development of the course, I made a plan for each unit that created space to introduce key literary terms that emerged within each unit's texts, as shown in Figure 2.2. After receiving Mr. Colombo's approval, we organized the class syllabus in preparation for teaching the course.

Figure 2.2. Literary Terms

Roots of Hip-Hop & Literature	Love	Family	The Hood	Politics	Despair
Allusion	Point of View	Mood	Rhyme Scheme	Assonance	Allegory
Signifyin(g)	Simile	Tone	Internal Rhyme	Consonance	Irony
Metaphor	Hyperbole	Imagery	Personification	Alliteration	
Plot	Theme	Analogy	Foreshadowing	Hyperbole	

Teaching Hip-Hop Lit

The day before the first official day of classes, Mr. Ormond approached Mr. Colombo and me and asked if we would have a problem with him adding students to our class. Although the enrollment sheet indicated that 20 students were registered, many more had requested to be added to what was being called "hip-hop class." We happily agreed to accept as many students as the classroom could comfortably hold and the school district would allow. On the first day of class, 35 students were waiting for us when we entered the classroom. Within 2 weeks, 20 students remained on the active attendance roll. These students, to varying degrees, formed the core of the Hip-Hop Lit community.

Like the rest of the Twilight Program, Hip-Hop Lit was a racially and ethnically diverse space. Of the 20 students enrolled in the course for the entire semester, 4 students were White, 3 Cambodian, 2 Latino, and 11 African American. Several students were added to the course at the midway point of the school year, all of whom were African American. The class's gender distribution was also consistent with the rest of the program, with 8 male students and 12 female students enrolled in the class.

With the exception of two people (Anita and Robin, the two oldest students in the program, who were 22 and 23 years old), the students were between 16 and 19 years old. Most of them were former HHS day school students and already had preexisting relationships with either Mr. Colombo or me. Seven of the 12 female students and one of the 8 male students in the class indicated that they had children. Although student attendance was a constant concern of Mr. Colombo and mine, most of the core group of Hip-Hop Lit students attended 3 days per week, which was significantly higher than every other course in the program.

Classroom Configuration

Unlike the other classrooms in the Twilight Program and most of the day school, Hip-Hop Lit was designed to encourage a feeling of community, facilitate storytelling, and discourage lecture-based teaching. To do this, the students, Mr. Colombo, and I converted the rows of classroom desks into a circle at the beginning of class and returned them to their original formation at the end of class in order to satisfy the teacher from whom we borrowed the classroom. I positioned the video camera behind the circle in order to be less intrusive and distracting to the other members of the class.

Rules

Due to the age of the students and our commitment to creating a more democratic space, Hip-Hop Lit operated with few preestablished rules. The most explicit and strictly enforced rule that we established was that stories shared within the class were not to be shared with anyone outside the class. We also emphasized the importance of respecting everyone's stories and opinions by not laughing, teasing, antagonizing, or being overly intrusive. Other class rules were negotiated by the students, Mr. Colombo, and I during the first few classes of the year and at various points throughout the year as issues emerged. Although school and program rules prohibited food in the building, we collectively agreed that students were permitted to eat their lunch or dinner to class provided they properly disposed of it. We also agreed to disregard the school's rules about bathroom usage ("No one can go to the bathroom except in-between classes or under extreme emergency and with the teacher's permission" [School District of Philadelphia, 2003, p. 13]) and decided that anyone could leave class for a "quick break" provided it wasn't distracting or disrespectful to other students. Profanity was permitted in class provided it was neither excessive nor abusive. Students were strictly prohibited from using what Mr. Colombo and I termed to be "hateful words" such as "nigger," "faggot," or "bitch" except when reading or commenting on a text. Despite the arbitrariness and potential for exploitation of the rules, students consistently honored their commitment to following what we established. This is a critical point, both for gaining a richer understanding of the context and to fully appreciate the reasons for the highly provocative, informal, and potentially offensive language that often appears in the data that I provide in this book.

Journal Writing

One of the central features of Hip-Hop Lit was journal writing. As students entered the class, they would retrieve their journal books from the milk crate that Mr. Colombo kept secured in his closet. For the first 10 minutes of each class, the students would write responses to a question that linked the day's topic to their own ideas and experiences. While some of the questions were fairly general (e.g., "What is love?" "What would be a good metaphor for your neighborhood?"), others, like the topics themselves, were extremely personal in nature (e.g., "Have you ever considered suicide?" "Have you or anyone you know been involved in an abusive relationship?"). During the journaling period, Mr. Colombo and I also responded to the question in our own journals.

Many of the students expressed a dislike for the journal-writing portion of the class. When asked why, nearly all of them indicated that although they were interested in the questions that were raised, they did not enjoy the act of writing. Consequently, many of these students deliberately came to class late in order to avoid journal writing. Others wrote very little in their journals and spent the time doing other things such as doodling, daydreaming, or pretending to write.

Journal Sharing

After the writing period ended, we asked the students to share their responses with the rest of the class. To begin the sharing portion, we asked a student to volunteer to read his or her journal entry. After the first response, we would ask each student in the circle to read his or her entry or, with more sensitive topics, request more volunteers. Under both circumstances, most of the students in the class offered some form of response to the question, even those who had written little or nothing in their journals. Mr. Colombo and I always shared our responses and frequently volunteered to offer ours first if the students were reluctant to speak.

Group Reading

After receiving a new text, the students would be given a few minutes to engage in sustained silent reading. Afterward, we would read the text out loud as a group. This was done because several of the students were not functional readers and I was not always confident that they would comprehend the entire text alone. Also, because we almost never listened to music in the course, group reading enabled the students to hear the lyrical complexity of many of the texts.

I would normally initiate group reading by reading the first few lines of the text and waiting for another member of the class to read the subsequent line. Since the process was entirely voluntary and unscripted, there were frequent moments when several students attempted to read a line simultaneously and other moments when no one was willing to read a line and Mr. Colombo or I had to read the majority of the text. Nevertheless, we continued to introduce texts in this way in order provide less skilled readers with the opportunity to listen to the text, read a line that was less difficult, or choose a line from the end of the text in order to practice reading it mentally before reading out loud. After completing our group reading, we would read the text again as a group or I would read it in its entirety for clarification purposes.

Reader Responses

After reading a text, the class would engage in various forms of reader response. This was done in order to help clarify and articulate ideas, share insights, and organize thoughts that emerged from our readings of the text within a group context. Our primary methods of reader response were informal written responses and text rendering. Each helped to facilitate a richer engagement with the course texts.

After reading the text, we would often engage in an informal (i.e., uncollected) writing assignment that asked us to respond to some portion of the text. Many of the questions were predetermined based on Mr. Colombo's and my lesson plan for the day. Others were developed within the class based on comments, emotions, or other things that emerged after the group reading. For some texts, the requested response was fairly broad, like "How did you feel about the text?" With other texts such as "Love is Blind," which deals with domestic violence, we asked more specific questions like "What memories come to your mind as you read this story?" After writing our responses, we shared them with one another. Depending on the degree of sensitivity, the informal responses were either mandatory or voluntary.

The most common form of reader response that we used in Hip-Hop Lit was text rendering, which is a reader response strategy in which readers of a text respond to a reading by reciting personally significant words, phrases, or sentences. This is done to delay initial response to texts and provoke thoughtful response (Robertson, 1990). After reading the text multiple times and taking a moment to reflect, everyone in the class was asked to write down a line or phrase and a word from the text that they found significant. Without comment, each person in the class would read the line or phrase that they selected until we returned to the first person. Then, without interruption, each person would read the word that they selected. After several minutes of silent reflection, we began to discuss and analyze both the text and our interpretations of the text rendering.

Formal Lesson

After the group discussion and reader response portions of the class, Mr. Colombo and I would shift into a more formal and guided analysis of the text and an introduction of key ideas that we wanted to discuss. At the beginning of the semester we began this part of the class by asking basic questions like "What was the main idea of the piece?" or "What was the author trying to say?" The remainder of the class time would be spent determining and debating the major themes of the text. As the semester progressed and students began to appropriate the language of formal critique that we were teaching, the questions and conversations became more complicated. For example, after reading "Suicidal Thoughts" by Notorious B.I.G. later in the semester, nearly the entire class quickly agreed that the text was intended as a suicide note and spent the remainder of the class analyzing the author's rhyme scheme and debating the presence of irony in his use of religious imagery.

It was my assumption at the beginning of the semester that I would frequently defer to Mr. Colombo's expertise as an English teacher and let him direct much of the lessons. For the first few lessons, the division of labor was fairly reflective of this expectation, as Mr. Colombo played an active role in teaching the lessons. Soon, however, he informed me that he "thought it would be better if you taught the lessons and I fill in the gaps when you need me" (informal communication, 10/9/03). I reluctantly agreed and led the lessons almost entirely myself for the remainder of the semester. At moments when I could not remember or did not know a concept, I would ask Mr. Colombo to take over and he would offer his assistance and return the class to me. This typically one-sided relationship, which is explicated throughout the book, is reflected in my ethnographic representations of Mr. Colombo as an ancillary and occasionally invisible figure within Hip-Hop Lit.

Unit Projects

At the end of each unit, students would be asked to construct individual or group projects that allowed them to provide a deeper response to the texts and make creative use of some of the literary strategies that they learned in the unit. These projects, which were completed entirely in class, forced the students to read or re-read the texts closely and work collaboratively. While students were resistant to working in groups at beginning of the semester, they soon grew to enjoy it and often requested (and were permitted) to work in groups even when assignments were deemed individual. The assignments for each unit are shown in Figure 2.3. After completing the assignments, individuals and groups would share their work with the rest of the class and submit it to Mr. Colombo and me for grading.

Final Project

The students were asked to complete a final project that would allow Mr. Colombo and me to further assess their emerging skills in literary interpretation. For the assignment, which was due on the last day of class, students were given the following options:

Figure 2.3. Unit Projects

Roots of Hip-Hop & Literature	Love	Family	The Hood	Politics	Despair
As a group, construct a story that either uses an extended metaphor and/or has a plot twist at the end.	Using lines from all of the texts that we've read, along with others that you find useful, "write" a piece that describes how you define love. (Note: It does not have to rhyme.)	Pretend you are Beanie Sigel and/or Jay-Z's father. As a group write a letter or rap in response to their songs.	Using the same style and rhyme scheme as an author from the unit, describe your neighborhood.	Imagine that you are running for president using the political beliefs of Nas and Dead Prez as your platform. As a group, construct a presidential speech that draws from "I Wanna Talk To You" and "They Schools."	Pretend you are writing an advice column. Create dialogues between the authors in the unit and you. Draw from the texts to determine their questions and use your own beliefs and opinions to provide the advice.

1. Select a text of your choice (minimum of 20 lines) and write a 1 to 2 page *typed* analysis paper. Using the skills and terms that you have learned during the course of the semester, you will briefly tell why you chose the text (the description should take up no more than half a page), describe what the text is about, and identify key literary terms and themes, including ones that you and/or your classmates have constructed this semester.
2. Create an original hip-hop text (minimum of 20 lines) and write a 1 to 2 page *typed* description paper. In this paper, you will describe your motivation for writing the text, as well as the particular literary strategies that you deliberately used, as well as those that you noticed after analysis. In addition to the 1 to 2 page paper, attach a type-written version of the text.
3. Develop and complete your own alternate assignment after discussing it with instructors.

To our surprise, nearly all of the students elected to complete the first assignment because it required less written work.

Grading

Student work was evaluated on a regular basis. At the end of each week, Mr. Colombo would grade students' journal entries. Grades were based on a "check," "check-plus," "check-minus" scale. Check-pluses were typically assigned to students who we considered to have made a good-faith effort to complete the day's entry. Check-minuses were given to students who made little or no effort to complete the task. Checks were usually reserved for students who completed the assignment late. Other class assignments were graded on a traditional "A, B, C, D, F" scale. Like the journal entries, this work was done entirely by Mr. Colombo, who felt that "if they come and work hard they should get an 'A.'" Given my educational philosophy that the assignment of letter grades is problematic, I agreed with his decision to adopt a liberal grading policy. At the end of the year, nearly all of the regular attendees received final grades of "A" or "B" in the class.

CONCLUSION

Howard High School provides an interesting context for this ethnographic study. An analysis of the various academic, economic, and social issues that HHS confronts enables a deeper understanding of the students who attended the school. It was this understanding that led me to conceive, co-construct, and co-teach Hip-Hop Lit within the Howard High School Twilight Program. As this chapter has demonstrated, Mr. Colombo and I deliberately constructed Hip-Hop Lit in order to facilitate various forms of storytelling and allow the students to develop literary interpretive skills through unconventional texts. Although the class had clear rules and boundaries, its structures enabled the unusual moments and "extraordinary conversations" (Fine & Weis, 2003) that I detail throughout the remainder of the book.

||||||||||||||||||||||||||||||||||||||||||||||||||||||||||||||||||||||||||||||||||||||||||||||||||

3

"Real Recognize Real"

Negotiating Authenticity Politics in Hip-Hop Lit

"Ethnicity, race, gender, class, sexuality, urbanity, and artistic proficiency are all enlisted to complicate others' claims to hip-hop authenticity in a geomusical game of cultural one-upmanship, a kind of high-stakes 'musical chairs' where participants scramble—once the beat stops—to shove themselves sagely atop one or another seat of definable, identity-based certainty."

—John L. Jackson, *Real Black*

"I put my hand on my heart, it mean that I feel ya real recognize real and you lookin' familiar"

—Jay-Z, "All Around the World"

A few days before the first day of class, Josh, a student from the Twilight Program, stopped me in the hallway and told me that he had just registered for Hip-Hop Lit. Before I could express my excitement, he asked, "Is this class gonna, like, be real? Or is it gonna be somethin' else?" Surprised by his question, I assured Josh that the class would be as organized and rigorous as any other course that was offered in the program. Playfully irritated by my response, Josh responded, "Nah, Hill. I'm not askin' if it's a real *class*. I'm asking if it's a *real* class, y'ah mean?" Although I assured him that I understood what he was saying, Josh accurately read my confused expression and continued explaining: "I know you a good teacher and everything but since the class is about hip-hop, I wanted to know if it's gonna be more *real*." At this point, Josh seemed satisfied that he had explained himself clearly enough for me to understand. Before I could probe further, Josh was pulled away by Mr. Ormond, leaving me only to speculate about the particular distinction that he was making.

In many ways, the curious mixture of ambiguity, specificity, and certainty that marked my exchange with Josh was a signpost of future conversations among members of the Hip-Hop Lit community. Throughout the school year, the term "real" and several of its variants operated as a floating signifier that indexed a variety of different meanings, preoccupations, and performances within the classroom. This chapter details the ways in which these conceptions of authenticity shaped students' engagement with various texts, themes, and processes within the course. Through the trope of "realness," students negotiated the course texts and one another in ways that enabled rich conversations and complex forms of identity work, but also presented formidable pedagogical and social challenges.

REAL HIP-HOP(PERS)

As new course texts were introduced, students would often engage in intense conversations about their authenticity. Specifically, the students discussed whether or not particular texts, as well as their authors, represented "real hip-hop." These conversations were typically led by three students, Joe, Gabe, and Ray, who positioned themselves as experts on hip-hop culture, as well as the arbiters of what constituted authentic hip-hop. These students referred to themselves as the "Hip-Hop Heads," or "Heads" for short. While they were not close friends outside of school, the Heads spent the bulk of their in-school time together, discussing the latest music or engaging in seemingly never-ending debates about "the Top-10 hottest MCs."

In addition to being hip-hop fanatics, the Heads were active graffiti artists, b-boys, DJs, and MCs. It was through these experiences that the Heads substantiated their authority on hip-hop culture. Joe, the only Head who was not Black, explains:

> A lot of people think they know what real hip-hop is but they
> don't. All that *fake* commercial stuff on the radio like Lil Jon
> and 50 Cent, that ain't hip-hop. That's rap. It's a difference,
> y'ah mean? Hip-Hop is the *real* stuff, the underground stuff, the
> grimy stuff. . . . Hip-hop is how we talk, what we wear, what
> we do by ourselves. The stuff they do ain't deep. It ain't even
> *real* art! [emphasis added]

As Joe's remark suggests, the Heads drew sharp distinctions of authenticity between the hip-hop music that they consumed and the commercial products enjoyed by their peers. As they often stated throughout the school year, the distinctions between "real" and "fake" hip-hop informed and reflected the Heads' understanding of their own roles within the classroom. These distinctions were consistently invoked as students encountered the course texts.

Identifying the Real

One of the primary ways that the Heads registered the authenticity of course texts was by drawing distinctions between "rap" and "hip-hop." Rather than merely echoing the many hip-hop scholars and critics who classify rap music as a distinctive "element" subsumed under the broader rubric of hip-hop culture (e.g., Pough, 2004; Rivera, 2003), the Heads articulated a more nuanced and refined framework that excluded texts that they deemed inauthentic. For them, the term "hip-hop" served as shorthand for "real" hip-hop texts, while "rap" was used, often pejoratively, for all texts that lay outside of their conceptions of authenticity. Like traditional modernist dichotomies between high and low culture (e.g., Adorno & Horkheimer, 1944; Arnold, 1932), the Heads' hip-hop/rap distinction was not merely informed by an analysis of particular texts, but by a belief about the capacity of particular sites of cultural production to yield authentic material. For the Heads, commercial rap artists like Lil' Jon and 50 Cent were not only inauthentic rappers, but representatives of an artistic field that was incapable of producing authentic material.

The Heads' rigid dichotomy between hip-hop and rap often shaped the ways that they analyzed and discussed course texts. For example, during a conversation about "I Wanna Talk to You," a political rap song written by Nas, Gabe described Nas as "one of them funny dudes, yo, 'cause he's a *hip-hopper* but he act like a *rapper* sometime." Conversely, commercial artists like Scarface were occasionally applauded for their ability to "flow like a hip-hopper . . . *sometime*." Rather than using such artists to complicate and ultimately reject their rigid hip-hop/rap binary, the Heads described them as exceptions to an otherwise useful rule: some people were real hip-hoppers and others were not.

The Heads' beliefs about what constituted authentic hip-hop, as well as the consequences of these beliefs, were most apparent when they engaged texts or authors that they believed were insufficiently authentic. For example, while journaling in response to "Love Is Blind" by Eve, Gabe wrote the following:

> As you already know, [I] normally have a lot to say about the texts. This time, it's hard, because Eve isn't a *real* hip-hop artist. She's a rapper. Next time, we should read something *real* like "God's Gift" by Jean Grae. [emphasis added]

Although he typically wrote long and thoughtful responses, Gabe argued that Eve, a commercially successful rap artist, wasn't worthy of his ordinary level of analysis. In addition to rejecting Eve, Gabe offered Jean Grae, a highly regarded underground hip-hop artist, as a more suitable (i.e., authentic) replacement. This is not to suggest, however, that the Eve text prevented Gabe from actively engaging the assignment. Rather, it prompted him to devote his energy to writing about why he could not write about Eve. Such behavior was common for the Heads, who were always engaged but consistently drew attention to their ostensibly refined taste in hip-hop music by rejecting anything that they did not assess as "real."

The Heads' beliefs about authenticity were most apparent when they were responsible for choosing texts for the class. While most students brought in songs from popular commercial artists like Beanie Sigel, Jay-Z, Tupac, Lil' Jon, and 50 Cent, the Heads almost always brought obscure work from these artists or, more typically, relatively unknown songs from underground hip-hop artists. As Ray, one of the Heads, explained, such practices were central to their perceived role in the classroom:

> We be bringin' that hot shit to class so they could know about real hip-hop. Like, when it's my turn to bring something in, I'm not gonna bring Tupac because everybody already know Tupac. If I do bring Tupac, though, it gotta be some shit they ain't never heard before. But most of the time, I'm gonna bring some slick shit like Immortal Technique, Dr. Octagon, or Bahamadia. If we don't do that, how else they gon' learn about real hip-hop?

As Ray's comment suggests, the Heads saw themselves as experts who were tasked with the responsibility of identifying and educating their peers about "real" hip-hop. This required them to expose their peers to texts with which they were presumably unfamiliar, both by familiar and unknown artists. Also, as the Heads often expressed to me privately, Hip-Hop Lit represented the first formal schooling space where they could assume such a welcomed leadership role. For this reason, they were particularly vocal in advocating and defending their positions on authenticity.

Challenging the Real

Although the Heads were generally well liked and respected by their classmates, their conceptions of "real" hip-hop were often challenged by other members of Hip-Hop Lit. The strongest opposition came from the other male students in the class, many of whom offered a sharply different conception of realness. For them, authentic hip-hop was not the province of the underground, but the "street." As Josh explains:

> [The Heads] be listening to that underground stuff. That stuff a'ight, but it ain't *real*. It ain't street. The dudes that be makin' that underground stuff be spinnin' around on they heads and livin' in the suburbs. They not from the 'hood. They more like White boys. The real shit come from niggas on the block, like [Beanie] Sigel, Freeway, and [Jada]kiss, feel me?

For students like Josh, the hip-hop celebrated by the Heads was insufficiently authentic because it was not produced by "niggas on the block," or Black and brown youth from urban neighborhoods. This position stood in sharp relief to the Heads, who tended to dismiss such artists, as Joe did in the earlier quote, as "commercial," "fake," and ultimately unworthy of their attention. An example of this tension came during the "Politics" unit, when Maggie brought in an early bootleg (pirated copy) of "Why" by Jadakiss. Although Jadakiss is a well-respected commercial artist known for making songs about guns, drugs, and consumerism, "Why" was widely acclaimed for its intensely critical examination of contemporary American culture. Despite the song's provocative and insightful commentary, Joe and Gabe quickly dismissed the text as "not real." The following exchange between Joe, Gabe, and their classmates illustrates the tension between the Heads and their peers:

Joe: This is wack. We should be reading "Nature of the Threat"
    by Ras Kass.
Gabe: Word. Gimme something real instead of wasting time
    with this "Why" shit.
Josh: Why y'all always saying something is wack? Joe, ain't you
    the one saying that street niggas don't be sayin' nothing?
    'kiss is spittin' some deep stuff right here. Why you hatin'
    on this one?
Joe: Ain't nobody hatin'. I'm just sayin'. . .
Me: I don't understand, Joe. Why don't y'all like this one?
Gabe: I'm just sayin', Hill. It's better stuff.
Me: OK, but if we look long enough, we could probably always
    find something that we think is better. What specifically
    don't you like about "Why?"
Gabe: I'm just sayin'. It's realer stuff. Not rap, but hip-hop.
Joe: Exactly.

This exchange is reflective of a recurring pattern within Hip-Hop
Lit. Although the Heads had well-developed and clearly articulated
positions about what constituted an authentic text, they were often
reluctant to acknowledge the legitimacy of artists who complicated
the "real/fake" dichotomy that they often appealed to when assessing
texts. For the Heads and their challengers, such assessments focused
less on the content of particular texts, but the particular label that
was assigned to the texts. In this case, the explicitly political nature of
"Why" was subordinate, if not altogether insignificant, to their understanding of Jadakiss's authenticity. This circumstance does not mean,
however, that the students were unaware of the complexity and contradictions of the real/fake dichotomy, nor that they were incapable of
negotiating them. Rather, it suggests that an analysis of their textual
commitments cannot be exhausted at the level of pure taste, but also
warrants an examination of the identity work that also shaped their
classroom practices.

Performing the Real

In addition to their classroom conversations, the Heads found other
ways to highlight their role as "real hip-hoppers." Nearly every day, the
Heads could be found wearing some combination of baggy jeans, sweatsuits, oversized "hoodies," 1980s retro t-shirts, Timberland construction boots, and suede Puma or shell-toe Adidas sneakers. Additionally,

although none of them were from New York, the Heads often slipped in and out of faux New York accents and regularly punctuated their sentences with New York-centric hip-hop slang like "son," "yo," and "B." According to Ray, the Heads's fashion and linguistic choices were "what we would be doing anyway, but we definitely add a little extra in class to separate ourselves from the others." Such maneuvers were not lost on their classmates, who often commented on the Heads's extravagant displays of hip-hop authenticity.

While most students playfully teased the Heads for being, as one student said, "hip-hop down to the socks," others found their performances to be problematic. As Keisha remarked:

> [The Heads] cool and everything but they act like they know everything about hip-hop. Anytime we say we like something, they be like [in a fake British accent] "that's not good enough. You don't know what you're talking about. Try this."

Keisha's use of a faux British accent, which is often equated with both cultural refinement and snobbishness, not only speaks to perceptions of elitism in relation to the Heads, but also the sense that there was something disingenuous about their performances. This notion was confirmed by the Heads themselves:

> *Me*: Why y'all be so rough on people that don't like what y'all like?
> *Gabe*: We gotta be, Mr. Hill. We tryin' to school people on real hip-hop. We gotta expose that fake shit.
> *Me*: I'm saying, though. Y'all be actin like y'all don't like nothin' they bring in.
> *Gabe*: It's not that. I like some of the stuff but . . .
> *Ray*: Me too. Like, I feel Biggie and Pac. [lowering his voice] I even like some of that crunk stuff.
> *Me*: *Crunk stuff*? Let me find out you like Lil Jon!
> *Gabe*: [laughing] We both like *some* of it. But if we was to admit it, we'd lose our hip-hop credentials.
> *Ray*: [laughing] Exactly!

As their comments suggest, the Heads's aesthetic commitments were not only driven by personal taste, but by a desire to reaffirm their identities as "real" hip-hoppers. This desire often led the Heads to misrepresent or understate their appreciation for texts that contradicted their elitist postures. For example, in the above conversation with Ray and Gabe, both of them acknowledge (outside the purview of their classmates) that they have an appreciation for "crunk music," a highly commercial form of Southern rap music popularized by artists like Lil Jon. Within the classroom, however, the Heads consistently referred to crunk music as unworthy of their attention, or as a "bad object" (Ang, 1985) that they only consumed to note how bad it is. As Gabe explained, these decisions were deliberately done to protect their "hip-hop credentials," or affirm their roles as experts on authentic hip-hop by demonstrating appropriately refined taste.

Such moves are theoretically illuminated by Bourdieu (1984), who argues that taste is not the result of an objective interpretation per-formed by a disinterested observer. Instead, it is the result of particu-lar "distinctions" that not only mark the object of analysis, but also the individual making the distinction. In Hip-Hop Lit, the Heads's authenticity performances became a means by which to affirm and assert their own in-school and out-of-school identities as authentic members of a hip-hop community. These practices were legitimated through the Hip-Hop Lit curriculum, which was undergirded by sim-ilar distinctions.

Canonizing the Real

Throughout the semester, I used the Heads's words and actions as a point of entry into a variety of critical classroom conversations. In particular, I used the debates regarding authentic hip-hop as teachable moments in which to talk about the politics of the Western literary canon, as well as the histories of particular genres of literature and music. Through these conversations, students were able to study how cultural products like Shakespearean plays and early jazz records have shifted from maligned popular culture texts to highbrow pieces of the American cultural canon. By discussing the processes through which cultural texts shift from popular to classic, the students were able to identify the arbitrariness of canonicity, as well as call into question their own conceptions of cultural authenticity.

As I attempted to challenge the students (particularly the Heads), I was forced to recognize my own role in reinforcing the very hier-archies that I was encouraging them to dismantle. This became clear toward the end of the semester, as I was challenging the Heads on their highbrow sensibilities:

Me: You don't see any difference between the ways that y'all reject certain kinds of hip-hop and the ways that people reject hip-hop?

Ray: I see what you saying but, I . . .

Dorene: Hold up, Mr. Hill. They not the only ones that be doing that.

Me: What do you mean, Dorene?

Dorene: This class do the same thing!

Me: Say more about that. How . . .

Gabe: Yeah, this whole class is more about what we like than what they like!

Keisha: Exactly!

Me: What do you mean? Half the stuff we read, I don't even like!

Khaleef: Yeah. The stuff *we* bring in. [class laughs]

Prior to this conversation, I had not considered my similarities to the Heads, both from my own perspective and that of the other members of the class. Like the Heads, I felt a need to expose the class to texts that I deemed more interesting and sophisticated. Although I had a slightly broader conception of the hip-hop canon than the Heads—for example, I considered Nas and Jay-Z exemplars of hip-hop artistry and intellect—I nonetheless made a conscious decision to include certain texts and exclude others based on my own standards of authenticity. After reviewing the curriculum, I realized that nearly all of the songs that I selected were written by artists who not only reflected my personal tastes, but neatly fit within the boundaries of what I deemed real hip-hop. Even curricular outliers like The Fresh Prince and N.W.A. had penned songs ("Summertime" and "Fuck tha Police") that I considered essential titles within the hip-hop canon.

My choices were reflective of a broader tendency within many HHBE contexts documented in the research literature. Typically, HHBE educators choose texts that they deem politically, intellectually, or culturally sophisticated and relevant. While appropriate, such moves often lead to the development of curricula that respond to the interests, experiences, and generational orientation of the teacher rather than the student. In doing so, HHBE contexts not only risk becoming less "culturally relevant," they can also replicate the very structures of elitism that HHBE contexts aim to problematize and ultimately dismantle.

REAL NARRATIVES

Given the course's focus on literature, as well as hip-hop culture's link to the African American storytelling tradition (Perry, 2004), a large portion of Hip-Hop Lit's texts took the form of narratives. Drawing from their interpretations of the texts, as well as their broader relationships with hip-hop culture, the students engaged particular types of narratives in ways that produced and reflected a complex range of authenticity politics.

Local Narratives

Many of the course texts reflected what Forman (2002) calls the "extreme local," or hip-hop's narrative preoccupation with specific cities, area codes, neighborhoods, housing projects, and so forth within its texts. Throughout the semester, students consistently expressed a preference for texts that emphasized geographic specificity and local knowledge. For example, texts from artists like Nas and Jay-Z provided considerable information about their respective lives in the Queensbridge and Marcy Housing Projects in Queens and Brooklyn, New York. When engaging such texts, many students, even those who were usually less engaged or talkative, became more active in classroom activities. As Khaleef explains:

> The stuff we be readin' get us talking 'cause it's more *real* than other stuff. . . . Like, I can tell that it really happened to [the authors] because they tell us where they from and stuff about they 'hood. Plus the [stuff] they be goin' through is the same as we go through. [emphasis added]

Khaleef's comments highlight two critical points. First, texts that represented the "extreme local" enhanced their believability ("it's more real"), which was a critical factor for increasing student motivation and engagement. Also, Khaleef's comment, which was echoed by many students throughout the semester, speaks to the importance of hip-hop narratives for humanizing urban experiences by appending names and faces to otherwise distant and abstract narratives about urban ghettos (Hill, in press). As critical race theorists have argued (e.g., Delgado Bernal, 2002; Guinier & Torres, 2002; Ladson-Billings, 1998), such narratives enable oppressed people to recognize the commonality of their experiences.

In addition to valorizing local narratives, students showed a particular affinity for texts from their hometown of Philadelphia. Some of the local narratives that the students most appreciated came from Beanie Sigel, a well-known rap artist from South Philadelphia. Sigel, whose rap moniker is a reference to his childhood home on Sigel Street, frequently includes references to local events, landmarks, and slang in his lyrics. As Keisha explained, such references provided particular value for the students:

> When we be readin' Beans and them, we like it because we could see ourselves in it. . . . I mean, I don't even like what Beans be rapping about with all the guns and drugs and stuff. But still, when he be droppin' our slang or talking about what be happening on Sigel Street, it's like we can see ourselves in the story. We can't never do that with regular stuff, even the Black stuff.

As Keisha explained, the significance of local narratives extended beyond the superficial value of seeing familiar sites and sounds. Rather, local narratives reflected what Dyson (2002) refers to as "Africeture," or the practice of people of African descent writing themselves into existence. Through the texts, students were able to see themselves as individuals worthy of representation within the public sphere. This point was elaborated by several students at the end of the school year:

> *Jay*: When we would read [local narratives], I get hype 'cause that's my hood. Like, when Freeway and Beans and them be rapping about my hood I know the whole world gonna know about the shit that I go through.
> *Me*: Why is that important to you?
> *Josh*: 'Cause people gonna know we exist. A nigga in Compton ain't never been to South Street or the Gallery but they gonna know about it from the rappers.
> *Jay*: Plus, niggas gonna know our hood is real too!
> *Keisha*: Yeah, like, don't nobody care about your 'hood till someone else rap about it.

For the students in Hip-Hop Lit, local narratives not only provided a space for them to "see themselves" in the texts, but also certified the "realness" of their neighborhoods and experiences to the broader public.

Cautionary Narratives

Many of the texts that were included in the Hip-Hop Lit curriculum were cautionary narratives. Classic hip-hop texts like "Love's Gonna Get'cha" by KRS-One and "Children's Story" by Slick Rick, which were brought in by students, as well as newer ones like "I Refuse Limitations" by Goodie Mob, were examples of such narratives. Each of these texts followed the standard pattern of cautionary narratives: a problematic choice is identified within the story; a character makes the problematic choice; and, as a result of that choice, a character meets an undesirable fate. For example, in "I Refuse Limitations," Cee-Lo (from the group Goodie Mob) chooses to sell drugs as a means of escaping poverty and limited employment opportunities. As a result of his choice, he is arrested and convicted, leaving his girlfriend and child to fend for themselves. Such stories often appealed to the students based on their resonance with their own lived experiences:

> *Maggie*: A lot of times I can learn from these stories more than
>   other stuff.
> *Me*: Why is that?
> *Maggie*: Because they situations is so real that I can relate more.
> *Khaleef*: Exactly, like when Cee-Lo talk about trying to eat
>   but not wanting to work at McDonald's, I could feel that
>   because I been through that.
> *Maggie*: And that makes it easier to take they advice.

As this exchange indicates, students often viewed the "realness" of the situations as the predicate for their engagement with the narratives.

In addition to increasing engagement with the texts, our discussions about cautionary narratives created space for the students and me to engage in critical media pedagogy. In particular, the narratives prompted the students to reflect upon the role of other cautionary texts within their daily lives:

> *Lisa*: Now that I think about it, we be seeing cautionary tales all
>   the time. Like back in the day on TV. Remember *Saved by the*

Bell, when the White girl started taking caffeine pills and got all messed up? That was a "cautionary tale," right? [class laughs]

Maggie: Yeah. It's like every time you watch a show, they have a special episode about something.

Josh: Yup, and back in the day they used to show them videos in school about not crossing the train tracks. Dude got smashed! [class laughs]

Ray: Yeah, yo, it seem like everybody always trying to "cautionary tale" us. [class laughs]

Me: Why do you think that is?

Maggie: 'Cause they think we a problem!

Me: Is that the only reason? What about having sincere concern for your well being? Like . . .

Lisa: I hear you, Mr. Hill. But why they always got to scare you into doing stuff?

Such conversations were common, as students were able to engage particular cautionary narratives, as well as engage in metalevel analyses of their role in daily life.

In addition to traditional cautionary narratives, texts such as "Ms. Fat Booty" by Mos Def and "Manifest" by The Fugees, which did not follow the traditional framework, were still viewed by the students as "cautionary" because of the undesirable outcomes experienced by the characters. In both texts, the narrator negotiates a broken heart after dealing with a duplicitous lover. Such texts were often preferred by the students, as they were seen as less contrived and didactic (i.e., more real) than traditional cautionary texts. As Kia explained, "Some of the stories basically be like 'the moral of the story is . . . '. Those is cool, but I like the ones better where we could find our own 'moral of the story.'" In finding their own "moral of the story," students subverted the logic of traditional literary interpretation and crafted new types of cautionary narratives based on their own conceptions of realness. One of the primary sites for this process involved narratives that contained material that Mr. Colombo and I found objectionable.

As discussed earlier, each of the units included texts that were brought in by the students. Although we allowed a wide range of relevant texts, even those of which we were not particularly fond, Mr. Colombo and I often challenged the students to explain the logic and significance of their choices. (It is worth noting that Mr. Colombo, who rarely participated in classroom teaching or conversation, was extremely active when challenging the appropriateness of student-selected texts.) Most often, we raised concerns about the problematic choices made by characters within the narratives, most of whom were not "punished" in the same matter as cautionary tales. When the students were challenged, however, they typically appealed to the cautionary nature of the texts in order to substantiate their significance. For example, Shaheem attempted to bring in Tupac's "Hit em Up" during the neighborhood unit. When I resisted this choice based on the text's wanton violence, the following exchange occurred:

> *Me*: I don't see how this text fits the neighborhood unit. Plus it's way too violent.
> *Shaheem*: That's why I like it. Not the violence but, like, you can see how Pac was wildin' out before. Then he learned his lesson.
> *Me*: He got killed!
> *Shaheem*: Exactly. So you can learn what happens when you start wildin' out and not listening to nobody!

Such examples were common, as students drew from their knowledge of popular culture, and more especially the lives of certain artists, in order to transform ostensibly ordinary texts into cautionary narratives. Although many texts, such as "Hit em Up," were still rendered inappropriate for class, they nonetheless exposed how students' connections to hip-hop texts created new possibilities for interpretation and understanding.

Oppositional Narratives

Many of the texts in Hip-Hop Lit were *oppositional narratives*, or stories in which the characters resisted, often successfully, dominant authority and norms. This was reflected in the number of oppositional narratives that the students selected and closely engaged throughout the semester. As hip-hop scholars (Cobb, 2007; Osumare, 2007; Perry, 2004) have noted, such texts are part of a broader tradition of oppositional figures within African American culture. The two most prominent figures in this tradition are the "trickster" and the "badman," both of which emerged out of precolonial African folk traditions (Roberts, 1989). While both characters represent oppositional figures, each operates in different ways: the trickster survives the dangers of the world through cunning, deceit, and clever manipulation of the law; the badman shows wanton indifference to rules, law, or morality (Abrahams, 1970; Roberts, 1989). The students' connection to oppositional figures became clear both through their written work and classroom discussions. Among the most popular narratives within Hip-Hop Lit were those by Jay-Z, Tupac, and 50 Cent.

In addition to the three Jay-Z texts that I selected for the class, students often made reference to and requested to bring in Jay-Z texts throughout the semester. While the students enjoyed the preselected course texts, all of which dealt with sociopolitical issues, they tended to prefer other texts in which Jay-Z bragged about his lyrical talents ("What They Gonna Do"), wealth ("I Love the Dough"), and former success as a drug dealer ("Friend or Foe"). According to many of the students, their connection to these texts was linked to Jay-Z's ability to sidestep the law, as well as societal expectations of African American youth. As Jay, who brought in "What They Gonna Do," explained:

> *Jay*: I like the fact that Jay-Z talk that ish for real. ["ish" is a euphemism for "shit"]
> *Me*: What do you mean?
> *Jay*: Like, he always come out on top. He moved weight [sold drugs] and didn't get locked up. He flipped it and got his own label, clothes, everything. Plus he brag about it and can't nobody do nothing. They can't get 'em. That ish is real!

Jay's observations demonstrate Jay-Z's role as a modern trickster figure, constantly outsmarting authority (both the criminal justice system and White corporate gatekeepers) and bragging about his exploits. This sensibility was articulated by the students throughout the semester, as they constantly made references in their writing and classroom conversations to Jay-Z's trickster maneuvers. For example, during a conversation about "Fuck Tha Police" by N.W.A., students make reference to Jay-Z's "99 Problems," in which Jay-Z outwits an overzealous patrolman:

> *Kristina*: I know how [N.W.A.] feel about the police but they could handle it differently.
> *Jay*: What you mean by that?
> *Kristina*: I'm saying, like, Jay-Z don't like the police either but he doesn't cuss them out.

Jay: Yeah, he know his rights and he don't let 'em lock him up.
Me: You mean like in "99 Problems"?
Jay: Exactly. Jay be like . . . [several students join in unison]
    "You gon' need a warrant for that!" [class laughs]

Also, during the despair unit, Dorene wrote the following journal response to Notorious B.I.G.'s "Suicidal Thoughts":

> In Suicidal Thoughts B.I.G. is tired of living because things isn't going write [sic] in his life. He felt like he could not beat the odds like Jay-Z and make it big.

Such examples show how Jay-Z is not only referenced frequently, but also invoked as a metaphor for defying authority, exceeding societal expectations, and achieving success.

In addition to Jay-Z, students regularly asked to bring in texts from Tupac and 50 Cent, both of whom had received considerable media attention for their encounters with law enforcement and gun violence. As with Jay-Z, the students' connection to 50 Cent and Tupac extended beyond the course curriculum, which included only one song from Tupac and none from 50 Cent, and into their broader out-of-school engagement with the rappers' lives. While the students were extremely familiar with Tupac, who was murdered in 1996 but had maintained a strong public presence through a string of posthumous albums, movies, and books, the students knew considerably less about 50 Cent, who had just released his commercial debut album during the first semester of Hip-Hop Lit. Nevertheless, the students frequently drew from each artist's work and biography, often conflating the two, at various points throughout the semester.

While the students celebrated Jay-Z for his ability to escape the strictures of society through cleverness and wit, they found equal pleasure in 50 Cent's and Tupac's willingness to unabashedly disregard the rules and mores of mainstream society. During the aforementioned conversation about "Hit em Up," Shaheem and Gabe offered the following explanation:

> *Shaheem*: I love [Hit em Up] because 'Pac is so real!
> *Me*: What do you mean by 'real'?
> *Shaheem*: He don't care about the law. He just be mashing!
> *Gabe*: Yeah. 'Pac was the realest to ever do it. It was bigger than

music with him. Gun shots, cops, couldn't nothin' stop him
from doin' his thing.

Me: Nothing? Pac got killed!

Shaheem: Pac ain't dead, Mr. Hill! He on a island somewhere
ducking the mafia and the feds. [half of the students laugh,
while others gasp in dramatic exasperation]

Through his confrontations with police and rival rappers (which he
details in the battle rap "Hit em Up"), Tupac represented the classic
outlaw figure who successfully confronts mainstream authority, rival
peers, and various forms of violence. Even Tupac's death, which I mentioned in response to the students' claims of invincibility, was countered with the popular urban legend that Tupac had not died, but had
once again escaped death (see also Dimitriadis, 2001, and Dyson, 2001
for similar analyses among different youth). Similar sentiments sur-
rounded 50 Cent, whom the students often viewed as the heir apparent to Tupac's legacy of outlawry. During every unit, students would
ask to bring in 50 Cent texts for class. While this was largely due to his
popularity–based on record sales and media exposure, 50 Cent was the
most popular music artist in the world at the time—it was also linked
to 50 Cent's construction as an oppositional figure. Kia explains:

> I like 50 Cent because he look good and he could rap and
> everything. But I really like him cause he be like "F the haters,
> the police, everybody." Just like 'Pac.

In a different conversation, Gabe, one of the Heads, added:

> I can't always mess with 'Pac and 50 Cent on the music tip, but
> I'll always check for them, especially 'Pac, 'cause they be on
> that real thug stuff. Not just killing niggas, but saying "F the
> system."

It was these sentiments that prompted the students to construct Tupac
and 50 Cent, as well as Jay-Z, not only as oppositional figures, but
heroes. As Roberts (1989) notes, the hero is not a universal character type, but the result of a process in which members of a particular
group create "figures who, from our vantage point on the world, ap-
pear to possess personal traits and/or perform actions that exemplify
our conception of our ideal self" (p. 1). For many of the students in

Hip-Hop Lit, oppositional figures like Tupac, 50 Cent, and Jay-Z were heroic figures because of their ability to challenge, subvert, and defy the forces and structures that they encountered on a daily basis.

Unlike local and cautionary narratives, which were celebrated for their ostensible "realness," the students enjoyed oppositional narratives precisely because of their contradictory relationship to the truth of their daily experiences. As Jay explained to me during a conversation about Tupac's encounters with gun violence:

> I mean, I know Pac shit ain't regular. I mean most niggas don't shoot cops, get shot theyself, and live to make tapes and shit. Most niggas just get locked up or die. But that's what make Pac so hot, y'ah mean? He did shit that niggas dream about but can't do!

In a different conversation about 50 Cent, Dorene added:

> I don't even be believing half that stuff. . . . I mean, I ain't saying 50 ain't get shot but he might overexaggerating. I mean, like, it might not *all* be true. But for real, though, it don't matter 'cause it's still decent that somebody could do that stuff.

As these comments suggest, the students' connection to oppositional narratives, as well as their construction of particular figures as heroes, was neither naïve nor uncritical. Rather than overestimating their truth value or replicability, the students used the narratives as a space to imagine and perform resistance to the threats and strictures of their lives.

REAL BLACKNESS

Based on the racial demographics of HHS and our experience with Black student attendance, Mr. Colombo and I planned to have more White and Asian students than Black students in the class. As a result, we designed the course with the expectation of having a racially and ethnically diverse audience. Although there were considerably more Black and fewer Asian students than we expected, our class was still relatively diverse on the first day of school. Despite this diversity, there was a sense within the school community that Hip-Hop Lit was, to quote Mr. Ormond, "demographically diverse, but *really* Black."

The truth of Mr. Ormond's statement became apparent very quickly, as multiple students, both Black and White, approached me during the registration period to find out whether or not White students were permitted to take the class. Also, despite the racial diversity of the classroom, students of all races frequently referred to Hip-Hop Lit as the "Black people class" or, among the Black students, simply "our class." While alternately playful and serious, these comments indexed the ways in which Hip-Hop Lit was imagined and discussed within the community as a Black space. This notion, which hinged upon particular conceptions of racial authenticity, radically reorganized the ways in which students understood and performed a range of classroom identities.

Authentic Black Space

Beliefs about the racial architecture of the class were directly linked to the students' beliefs about the racial essence of hip-hop culture. Throughout the school year, students consistently argued that hip-hop culture was quintessentially Black, thereby rendering our class a Black space. This point was frequently offered not only by students in Hip-Hop Lit but outsiders like Darius, a Twilight student who was not in the class:

> *Darius*: Anybody can take y'all class but you could tell that it's for Black people.
> *Me*: Why do you say that? There's all kinds of people in the class.
> *Darius*: Yeah but it's a rap class. It's a hip-hop class. Not heavy metal! [laughs]
> *Me*: [laughing] Who likes heavy metal around here? Don't nobody like metal!
> *Darius*: You know what I'm saying, Mr. Hill. The White people *here* might not like that stuff. They might even like hip-hop. Still that don't mean it's not a Black people class. Hip-hop is Black so it's a Black people class!

A similar notion was echoed by Keisha, a Hip-Hop Lit student:

> *Keisha*: I like how y'all made a class for us.
> *Me*: By "us" you mean . . .

> *Keisha*: Stop frontin', Hill. You now what I'm saying. [laughing]
> Colored people.
> *Me*: [laughing] Actually, I didn't think that many Black people
> would be here. Most of y'all don't be coming to class like
> that.
> *Keisha*: I know! But we coming 'cause it's for *us*. And don't act
> like you wasn't thinking that. Colombo too!

Although not always as explicit as Darius and Keisha, students inside
and outside the class frequently articulated the notion that the Hip-
Hop Lit curriculum was designed, intentionally or unintentionally, for
an audience of Black people. Such beliefs were not limited to students,
but also by teachers like Mr. Carrey, a White social studies instructor in
the Twilight Program:

> Don't get me wrong. I like what you're doing and everything
> and, obviously, you can't legally teach a class that White kids
> can't take. Still, it's kinda clear that if you're teaching a class
> about rapping, it ain't for the White boys [laughs], it's for the
> Black kids. I think it's good, though. They need their own class
> too, especially in a place like this. It's about time we got some-
> thing that speaks to them.

Although he did not understand the purpose of the class—like several
other teachers, he ignored my explanations and continued to describe
the course as a how-to workshop on rapping—Mr. Carrey nonetheless
saw Hip-Hop Lit as a more authentic fit for Black students than the
traditional curriculum. This notion was echoed by Black teachers like
Mr. Watson, who placed a handwritten note in my mailbox toward the
middle of the school year:

> I just want to thank you for doing something for OUR KIDS!
> It's about time somebody came to give us something *real*. [em-
> phasis added] The European curriculum just isn't going to give
> OUR kids what they need culturally to get them out of their
> situation. Good job my brother!

For Mr. Watson, a staunch advocate of Afrocentric education, Hip-
Hop Lit represented a more "real" (i.e., culturally relevant) approach
to teaching Black students than the standard Eurocentric curriculum.
Like many Afrocentric education scholars (e.g., Asante, 1991), Mr.

Watson's stance presumes the existence of an essential Black culture that transcends history, geographic location, and culture orientation (Appiah, 1992). While no one else in the school offered the same Afrocentric perspective, they nonetheless conceded the existence of an essential Black cultural form that could be appealed to through authentic curriculum and pedagogy. With regard to Hip-Hop Lit, the belief that hip-hop was an authentic product of Black culture prompted HHS teachers and students to view the class as a more "real" space for the program's Black students.

Deracializing Classroom Conversation

Although the racial dimensions of the curriculum were discussed in relatively explicit terms, conversations about race within the context of classroom pedagogy were far more ambiguous. Despite the prominence of themes related to race in the course texts, most students would avoid using explicit race labels during classroom discussions. Instead, they deployed terms like "culture," "urban," "street," and, most frequently, "hip-hop" as proxies for "Black." This practice stood in sharp contrast to their behavior in other classrooms, where students would willingly and voluntarily engage in explicit conversations about issues related to race and, more especially, Blackness. Consider, for example, the following conversation about "Dynasty (Intro)" by Jay-Z during our Despair unit:

> *Me*: To what is Jay-Z referring when he says "startin' to darken my heart, about to get to my liver"?
> *Lisa*: He talking about getting angry. His "heart getting dark" is saying that he's becoming a different person.
> *Joe*: Yeah, he's using imagery to talk about how he's becoming cold to the world.
> *Dorene*: Yeah. He had a hard life, like a lot of hip-hop people. Now he about to start drinking too!
> *Me*: You think he's talking about being a rapper?
> *Dorene*: No, not hip-hop like *that*. Like regular *hip-hoppers* in the street.
> *Robin*: Exactly. Hip-hop people don't have father figures and they gotta make it own they own.
> *Dorene*: Exactly. That's why he's dealing with, um , despair. Yeah, that's the word you be using. He speaking for hip-hop people.

A similar conversation occurred during our conversation about N.W.A.'s "Fuck Tha Police," as we linked the text to the broader tradition of Western protest literature:

> *Me*: What are some connections that you see between N.W.A. and our conversation about Ralph Ellison and John Steinbeck?
> *Maggie*: They're all talking about the problems in the world.
> *Me*: Can you say more about that?
> *Maggie*: Ummm. Well, I know with Ellison, he's talking about hip-hop people too!
> *Me*: Hip-hop? *Invisible Man* came out in the 1950s. I ain't see 50 Cent in there! [class laughs]
> *Maggie*: [laughing] Shut up Mr. Hill! You know what I mean.
> *Josh*: Yeah, like the same way that hip-hop people get beat up by the police now, people was getting treated messed up back then with Martin Luther King and them!
> *Maggie*: Exactly!!

These exchanges, which reflect typical instances of race talk in Hip-Hop Lit, enabled the students to discuss issues of race without explicitly invoking racial identifiers.

As several of the Black students explained to me, the tendency to sidestep explicit conversations about race was directly connected to their beliefs about Hip-Hop Lit as a Black space:

> *Keisha*: Sometimes, it's hard to talk about race because it can start trouble. When I talk about hip-hop and hip-hop people, it makes it easier.
> *Me*: Even if everybody knows what you're talking about?
> *Keisha*: Yeah, because "hip-hop" doesn't make people mad like the way they would if I say "Black people do this or Black people do that . . . "
> *Me*: But if everybody knows you mean Black people, how does it help?
> *Dorene*: I don't know, but it do! If I talk about colored people in class, White people might not feel right. But if I say "hip-hop," now everybody could talk about it.
> *Me*: Is this something that you do in all of your classes?

Keisha: Nah. In regular class you got to stand up for yours. But in here it's different.
Dorene: Exactly. It's hip-hop class so we gotta be more chill with it.

In a later conversation, Jay articulated this point more succinctly:

When you in a regular class, it's like a White class so you feel like you gotta stand up for Black people. When you in a Black class it's different. You don't want the [Whites] to feel uncomfortable *the way we do in their class* so we just talk around it. [emphasis added]

As these comments suggest, students not only understood Hip-Hop Lit as a Black space, but implicitly recognized their other classes as de facto White spaces. Rather than replicating the marginalizing practices of traditional classrooms, students decided to sidestep explicit racial discourse in order to create a more comfortable context for White students. Such efforts were not restricted to Black students, as the White members of Hip-Hop Lit also viewed the racialized nature of the classroom as prohibitive with regard to race talk. In fact, as I will discuss later, White students like Maggie and Kristina often expressed a more acute awareness of this dynamic than other members of the class:

Maggie: I'm not gonna talk about racial people in the same way that I do when I'm in a regular class.
Me: When you say "racial people" you mean . . .
Maggie: [laughing] You know what I mean. Like, [pauses for a moment, then resumes in a lower voice] Black people. Like in a regular class I could just talk. In here I can't.
Kristina: Yeah!
Me: But why? Do you think something's gonna happen?
Kristina: Not like that. I mean, we all cool. But when you in somebody else's house, you want to respect them. I feel like if I come in to this class talking about Black people, it's gonna be like, "Who is this White chick getting all racial?"
Maggie: Yeah, exactly. I like what we doing here and I don't want any drama because we start talking about Black people.

The students' avoidance of race talk reflects what Pollock (2004) refers to as "colormuteness," or the elimination of race labels during ordinary conversations. As Pollock argues, the suppression of racial markers within everyday discourse does not eliminate racial hierarchies, but masks the various ways that racial inequality functions within educational spaces.

In the case of Hip-Hop Lit, the existence of colormuteness made it more difficult to collectively engage the issues of race that emerged from many of the course texts, particularly at the beginning of the semester. Although I selected particular texts with the expectation that they would enable deep conversations about race, the notion that the class was an authentic Black space radically altered the ways in which racialized classroom discourse could be engaged. Consequently, classroom conversations often shifted away from direct conversations about race and more toward metalevel conversations about *how* we would talk about race. Although these challenges became less formidable as the students built a stronger sense of community—a process that will be detailed in Chapter Four—they nonetheless show how the notion of authentically Black space shifts the ways in which students understand their roles, rights, and responsibilities within the classroom.

Navigating Black Space

The notion that Hip-Hop Lit was an authentic Black space not only affected how students discussed race, but also shaped the more quotidian aspects of classroom pedagogy. In particular, Hip-Hop Lit became a space that enabled students to deploy symbols, styles, and practices that were marginalized in their other classes. For students like Jay, the notion of authentic Black space allowed the students to "act hip-hop." He explains:

> Acting hip-hop is like talking the way we talk on the block. It's like, y'ah mean, the way I'm talking right now. Like, I ain't gotta correct myself. I could just go. In regular class, if you act hip-hop, you get in trouble or the teacher act like you not smart. They'll tell you to "that's not how we act in here," but in here we could act hip-hop. We could act *real*. [emphasis added]

In another conversation, several students described Hip-Hop Lit as a place where they could be more real:

Josh: The thing about this class is that you could be more real.
   You don't gotta change how you talk you could be yourself.
Me: Are you not yourself in other classes?
Josh: I am [pauses] but it's different. I'm a different person. I'm
   not fake or nothing, but not as real.
Me: In what ways?
Gabe: Like, how you talk, how you walk. The shit you be
   talking about. It's different.
Josh: Exactly
Keneka: Like, I say what I want in any class. You know that!
   Still, it get treated different in here. Like, I could be more
   realer in here.

For these students, Hip-Hop Lit became a space in which they could behave in ways that they deemed more authentic. As Jay's notion of "acting hip-hop" suggests, particularly in light of the students' use of "hip-hop" as a proxy for Blackness, these notions of authenticity were deeply racialized. As such, students viewed Hip-Hop Lit as a space in which they could perform and validate particular conceptions of racial authenticity. One of the primary ways that this occurred was through the use and legitimation of what Carter (2005) refers to as "Black cultural capital," or nondominant (i.e., nonWhite, non–middle class) cultural signals within the classroom space. As Carter (2005) and Johnson (2003) argue, these forms of capital serve the instrumental purpose of forging intragroup solidarity and marking racial and ethnic authenticity.

One of the ways that Hip-Hop Lit privileged Black cultural capital was through the use of language. Within the classroom, the students used African American Vernacular English (AAVE) as well as Hip-Hop Nation Language (Alim, 2006) in ordinary classroom discourses. Although Standard English grammar and syntax were part of our grading rubric for students' written work, Mr. Colombo and I made a conscious decision not to "correct" their spoken grammar or syntax. The students' linguistic practices were further sanctioned through my own unconscious tendency to speak in AAVE as often as I spoke Standard English. According to the students, these conditions made students feel not only comfortable but compelled to speak in this way:

Michelle: Like, I talk hip-hop anyway, but in this class you *got to.*
Me: "Got to?" You act like we put it on the syllabus!

Michelle: I ain't sayin' all that but I ain't never had a class where
everybody talk like that. Usually you gotta *try* to talk White.
. . . I mean, not *White*. But, you know, like, the way school
want you to.

Me: I feel you.

Dorene: See! That's what we talking about. You "feel" me?
Don't no teacher be talkin' like that. That's why *we* talk like
that!

Me: I'm just talking like that right now. It's not like I do it all
the time.

Michelle: What? Is you serious?

Jay: I got your back and everything, Hill. But you the main one
that be talking like that.

Dorene: Exactly! But it's not just you. The whole class talk like
that. It's like if you don't talk like that you don't fit in. You
sound like a weirdo.

Kia: Exactly. I usually get props from my teacher for talking
proper in school. Now I don't even try. [laughing] You gets
nothing for that around here!

Another form of Black cultural capital that came through was knowledge of Black cultural reference points such as food, social experiences,
and music. Typically, these reference points would emerge during ordinary classroom discourse and extend into brief but spirited exchanges
about them. For example, during our reading of "Year of the Dragon"
by Wyclef Jean and Lauryn Hill, the following conversation occurred:

Alicia: I like how they be talking about old school stuff like
catching the cheese [school bus] and leather bomber jackets.

Me: What y'all know about leather bombers? When I was
young, we rocked 8-ball jackets.

Robin: Whatever. I know about them. Y'all remember Fila
boots?

Shaheem: Hell yeah! But, yo, Starter jackets with the football
teams on the back. What y'all know about that?

Me: I remember all that stuff! But let's look at the text closely.
What type of feeling do they want us to get from the text?
What's the mood?

Lisa: They want us to remember the good old days.

Me: Yes! Nostalgia . . .

This type of exchange was common in Hip-Hop Lit, as students would momentarily engage in playful forms of cultural one-upmanship that required intimate knowledge of particular aspects of Black culture. Similar conversations regularly occurred in relation to issues of poverty, teen pregnancy, fatherlessness, and experiences with violence, all of which were framed by students as tropes of Black authenticity:

> *Kia*: [A] lot of times, we start talking about stuff and it gets real.
> *Shaheem*: Yeah. I don't always talk but when it get real I come in.
> *Me*: And by real, you mean . . .
> *Shaheem*: When we start talking about niggas getting locked up or how [living in] the projects be all messed up. You know, the stuff that be in the stuff we reading in class.
> *Kia*: Yeah: That be real.
> *Me*: But what makes those things real? What if you don't know about those things?
> *Shaheem*: Then you not real! I mean, like, you could still listen and stuff but you really can't talk unless you been through it or know somebody real good that been through it. That's why White people get kinda quiet when we start talking about "real" shit. [group laughs]
> *Ray*: Word. Even some Black people can't talk about it!
> *Kia*: Exactly. Just 'cause you Black don't mean that you real! But, if you ain't Black you probably not real. I know that sounded all crazy, but you understand?

Such exchanges demonstrate how Hip-Hop Lit was not only imagined as a "Black space," but organized around particular and often stereotypical conceptions of Blackness. Although these conceptions created spaces for critical classroom conversation and facilitated effective pedagogy, they nonetheless delimited possibilities for how students could participate within the classroom community.

(Re)Negotiating Otherness

The formation of Hip-Hop Lit as a Black space not only created new possibilities for classroom identity work, but also new conceptions of "otherness" within the same space. By "otherness," I refer to the processes through which students came to feel like outsiders, what Said (1979) refers to as "alien," within the Hip-Hop Lit context. For some students, the classroom became an exclusionary space that pushed them (further) toward the social margins of the classroom. For others, it became a site of possibility for renegotiating their classroom identities in a variety of complex ways.

Within Hip-Hop Lit, there were four White students, Joe, Kristina, Lisa, and Maggie, who regularly attended class. Although each of them was knowledgeable about hip-hop culture (particularly rap music) and were friends with many of the Black students, they nonetheless expressed the feeling of being an outsider within the classroom. Ironically, it was at these moments that students were most explicit about their racial identity:

> *Lisa*: I mean, I love hip-hop and everything. I always did. But
>   I'm still a White girl, you know? Like, the same way that
>   a Black person could love the opera but it's still White, a
>   White person could love hip-hop but it's still Black. In here,
>   I'm still White.
> *Maggie*: Right. I mean, I love hip-hop but I can't *be* hip-hop so I
>   just play my position in here.
> *Joe*: I disagree. I *am* hip-hop, just like the Black people. But I still
>   play my position. It's still certain ways that I'm not *in*.
> *Kristina*: Exactly.

Despite their connection to hip-hop culture, as well as their relationships with other students in the class, each of the White students saw their racial identity as something that necessarily rendered them outsiders. They made sense of and responded to these feelings in a variety of complex and sometimes contradictory ways.

For Kristina, the sense of being an outsider shaped how she engaged in classroom conversations. Although she was very vocal during conversations about traditional literary themes, she became extremely quiet during conversations even tangentially related to race. This became apparent to me toward the middle of the semester, when I noticed that Kristina began to devote extra class time to journaling about topics that were discussed in the previous day's lesson. For example, she wrote the following entry in her journal the day after the class read "Year of the Dragon":

Yesterday, we were talking about back in the day. It made me think about when we used to go to the Chinese store and steal candy. I know it was wrong but it was fun and hey, we were kids right? ☺

When I asked Kristina why she didn't share her story during the previous day's class discussion, she replied:

I'm not gonna jump into a conversation if it ain't for me. Like, me and everybody are cool but I'm not one of the those White people that thinks they know everything about Black people, even if we're saying the same things. I just listen and do my work. If I got something important to say I'll say it, but usually I just don't say anything.

Although the comments from her journal were relevant to the previous day's conversation, Kristina nonetheless felt that the discussion "ain't for me." After recognizing this pattern, I began to call on Kristina during such discussions in order to encourage her contributions to the conversation. Although she would respond to me, her answers would be uncharacteristically short, or only vaguely connected to the topic of discussion.

Unlike Kristina, the other White students in the class responded to their feelings of otherness by attempting to deploy the same forms of cultural capital that the Black students used. For example, Maggie, Lisa, and Joe always used the latest slang and spoke in AAVE almost exclusively in class. They also made frequent references to the same cultural markers as the Black students in the class. For Maggie and Joe, these practices required little effort, as they grew up around and continued to spend considerable time with Black people. They explain:

Me: You two seem more comfortable in the class than some of the other White students.
Maggie: You mean the ones that don't be coming or you mean Lisa?
Me: Let's just talk about y'all for now.
Maggie: For me, all I hang around is Black people. My boyfriend is Black, my friends is Black, my music is Black. Not like Lisa!

Joe: Well, for me, I'm a hip-hop head so I'm always around
     Black people and I know everything about hip-hop. I can
     come in here and chill and be cool with everybody. It's not
     like I stop being White, but I become a little less White when
     I'm in here. At least for a minute. Just like when I'm doin'
     hip-hop.
Maggie: A little less White? [laughing] Yeah, I feel like I get a
     little less White every day!
Me: What does that mean?
Maggie: Like, I could just be myself. I'm not the average White
     girl.
Joe: Me neither.

For Maggie and Joe, Hip-Hop Lit became a space for them to become
"a little less White," or to engage in practices that enabled them to play
with their own conceptions and performances of racial identity.

Despite their comfort within Black spaces, Maggie and Joe also recognized the tacit boundaries of their participation. For example, students would occasionally engage in "bustin' contests"—playful forms
of teasing also known as "jawnin'" or "snappin'"—in ways that invoked race. In these moments, Maggie and Joe never contributed to
the exchanges and went to great lengths not to laugh. The following
exchange between Kwame and Keneka provides an excellent example
of this:

Kwame: Like Biggie said hisself, he was "Black and ugly as
     ever."
Keneka: I know you ain't talkin'. You Black as I don't know
     what.
Kwame: What? *I'm* Black? You look like the inside of a bookbag!

At this moment, everyone in the class laughs. Maggie and Joe cover
their faces to avoid being seen laughing.

Kwame: Yo, Joe. Ain't she Black?
Joe: I ain't got *nothing* to say about that.
Keneka: That's right, Joe. You down but you ain't *that* Black!
     [class laughs]
Maggie: I know that's right!

It was this tacit understanding of the boundaries of their participation that endeared Joe and Maggie to the Black students in the class. As Dorene explains, "Maggie and Joe is cool as shit. They act Black but they know they not Black. They *real*. They don't act like Lisa." In addition to averring the relative authenticity of Maggie and Joe, Dorene's comment reflects a general sense in the class that Lisa was less authentic than the other White students in the class.

Although she stated on multiple occasions that she viewed herself as an outsider who understood the racial boundaries of the class, Lisa often went to great lengths to perform as an insider. During the first week of class, Lisa wore a pendant bearing a photo of her 6-month-old biracial son. As she went around the room showing it to everyone in the class, she repeated several times, "This is my son. His dad is Black." When I asked her about this later, she said, "I just wanted everybody to know that I'm down with Black people, not White people."

In addition to speaking in AAVE and using slang—practices that appeared more forced for her than Maggie and Joe—Lisa frequently participated in the very same conversations that Maggie and Joe avoided. Rather than acknowledging Lisa's contributions, the students demonstratively ignored her remarks or stopped talking altogether. By the end of the semester, there was an unwritten rule among the students that Lisa's contribution to a conversation signaled the end of discussion. As soon as Lisa spoke, students would become dead silent for a few seconds before breaking into laughter. Although Lisa would laugh along with her classmates, she later confessed to me, "I don't know why they be clowning me all the time. I be saying the same stuff that they be saying. Sometimes it be funny but sometimes it hurt my feelings."

Lisa's failure to understand the boundaries of the class not only provided moments of levity, but occasionally produced real tensions in the class. The most extreme example came a few weeks after the exchange between Kwame and Keneka. Before the start of class, Lisa said to Kwame, "Damn, baby, why is you so Black?" Instead of initiating the playful exchange that she expected, most students remained silent and a few appeared visibly angry. The tension reached its peak when Dorene said, "Damn. Hip-hop class gonna get somebody ass beat!" Although I quickly defused the situation, Lisa remained upset for the remainder of the class and did not return for a week. When I asked her about the incident, Lisa said:

I'm not mad at Dorene or nothing. I guess I just went too far. I just figured that everybody knows that I don't mean anything bad. Like, I'm clearly not a racist. My son is Black, I talk Black, and we're in a doggone hip-hop class. I bet you they wouldn't have gotten mad if Maggie or Joe had said it!

From Lisa's perspective, her own performances of Black authenticity enabled her to participate in conversations and practices that otherwise would have been off limits. For the other students in the class, however, it was her failure to meet their standards of authenticity that rendered her an outsider. The day after Lisa's exchange with Kwame, the students discussed their feelings about her:

> *Josh*: We don't hate her. We just get mad 'cause she tries too hard.
> *Me*: I hear you, but I think you guys are hurting her feelings.
> *Dorene*: Well, it hurt my feelings when she be trying to act Black.
> *Me*: Maybe that's just how she acts. Maybe that's just her.
> *Kristina*: No it's not, Mr. Hill. We grew up together. She just started acting like that. Like Maggie is my friend too, but she always acted hip-hop. Lisa don't even talk like that outside of class. She only wears those big earrings in class!
> *Josh*: Yeah, she makes all White people seem corny. [class laughs]
> *Me*: Let me ask you a question. Would y'all have gotten mad if Maggie, Joe, or Kristina had called Kwame "Black"?
> *Kristina*: That's the point though. We wouldn't do that. We play our position.
> *Me*: But if you did . . .
> *Josh*: It would be different 'cause, even though they White, they still real.
> *Dorene*: I mean, I wouldn't like it. But I wouldn't trip 'cause I know where they comin' from.

For Lisa, the Hip-Hop Lit classroom represented an opportunity to experiment with her own conceptions of racial identity. Given the racialized nature of the space, Lisa was able to engage new ways of speaking, dressing, and functioning that reflected her desire to "try on" an authentic Black identity. It was these efforts, and the inevitable failures that accompanied them, that contributed greatly to Lisa's sense of otherness within the class.

Feelings of otherness were not restricted to the White students in the class. For some of the Black students, failure to satisfy the conditions of authentic Blackness made them feel unauthorized to fully participate in certain aspects of classroom life. For example, Michelle, a quiet African American student, completed all written assignments but rarely participated in classroom conversations. On a note attached to her final assignment, she offered the following explanation for her lack of participation:

> I think I should get an "A" in the class because I do all my work and I get good grades. I learned a lot in the class even though I don't talk a lot. It's not that I don't like the class. It's just that I grew up different so I don't know a lot of the stuff that they talk about . . . I'm not really hip-hop so I don't talk as much as I do in normal classes.

Although Michelle was not the only Black student to make such comments, she was the only one who regularly attended class. Others, like Greg, attended class sporadically and never participated in any assignments. At the end of the school year, he offered the following explanation:

> I felt like I was not Black enough for the class. I mean, I'm plenty *Black*. Look at me! (laughs) But in terms of the class, I don't talk Black enough or talk about the same stuff as y'all. I'm from Mt. Airy [a racially diverse middle-class section of Philadelphia] so I'm not really like them. I think the class is good for the people that are in there and everything but it's not for me. I don't really fit in.

While Greg's absence from class was not likely due to the racial dynamics of the class exclusively—he was in the Twilight Program because of excessive lateness and absence from day school—his notion of "not fitting in" nonetheless resonated with several other Black students in the class.

Understanding the notion of otherness that emerged within Hip-Hop Lit is critical for developing a more full and complicated understanding of the classroom, but also the broader tradition of culturally relevant pedagogy that theoretically undergirded the project. Rather than merely spotlighting the ways in which hip-hop–based education forges new cultural connections to previously marginalized groups, we must also keep track of the ways in which such interventions produce new cultural margins and, thus, new forms of marginalization. Also, by accounting for the complexity and fluidity of identity, we can begin to move beyond essentialist notions of culture and develop richer and more context-specific forms of curriculum and pedagogy.

III

Wounded Healers

Forming Community Through Storytelling

"No one can help anyone without being involved, without entering with [one's] whole person into the painful situation, without taking the risk of becoming hurt, wounded, or destroyed in the process . . . without a willingness to make one's own painful and joyful experiences available as sources of clarification and understanding . . . [T]he great illusion of leadership is to think that [humankind] can be led out of the desert by someone who has never been there."
— Henry Nouwen, "The Wounded Healer"

"This ain't no marketed music
People going through pain, I'm just talking 'em through it"
— Jay-Z, "You're Welcome"

In Greek mythology, Chiron, half-man and half-horse, was an extraordinary physician, teacher, and healer. One day, he was accidentally hit in the knee with an arrow from Hercules. Because the arrow was coated with the blood of Hydra, Chiron was unable to heal the wound that it opened. As an immortal, he could not die and was therefore forced to bear the pain of the wound while continuing the practice of healing. From that point forward, he became known as "the wounded healer." In this chapter, I detail how the articulation of personal narratives within Hip-Hop Lit produced a similar practice of "wounded healing," where people bearing the scars of suffering shared their stories in ways that provided a form of release and relief for themselves and others.

By wounded healing, I refer not only to the therapeutic dimensions of personal and collective storytelling, but also a critical engagement with majoritarian narratives that exposes and produces new possibilities. Through this practice, students formed a storytelling community in which membership was predicated upon an individual's ability and willingness to "expose their wounds" (share their stories) to the remainder of the group.

In this chapter, I continue to explicate the complex relationships that students forged with the course's hip-hop texts, many of which resonated with the students' lived experiences. I then illustrate how these relationships enabled classroom discussions and interactions from which the practices of wounded healing emerged. Finally, I highlight some of the dilemmas and tensions that emerged as Mr. Colombo and I attempted to privilege the stories and experiences of our students and ourselves within the classroom.

"I GOT A STORY TO TELL"

Although the students in Hip-Hop Lit expressed interest in the course from the beginning, they were generally reluctant to speak about their own personal experiences at the beginning of the school year. For the first month, classroom conversation was primarily limited to analysis of the course texts, with little explicit connection to students' personal experiences or stories. While this reluctance was partly due to the impersonal nature of our first unit, Roots of Hip-Hop and Literature, which contained only one autobiographical narrative, their discomfort with sharing personal information in front of strangers seemed to be the most important reason. As Jay later told me:

> It's like, at the beginning ain't nobody wanna talk . . . 'cause they ain't know nobody. You don't know who listenin' or what they gonna do. If my enemies is in here and I don't even know it, how I'm gon' tell them [something] that they could use against me? . . . But then it got cool when everybody started talking and it was like "oh, you gon' tell me this, then I'm gon' tell *you* this."

Dorene, Lisa, and Kristina were even more specific about when and why the class began to talk:

> *Dorene*: I know I wasn't gonna say nothin' if ain't nobody else say nothin'. I was like . . . "y'all ain't gonna be talking 'bout me when I leave." Then I remember Robin said something

about love and it was deep and then everybody wanted to start saying stuff.

Lisa: Exactly!!

Kristina: True!!

Lisa: When Robin started talking I felt like I could say whatever I had to say.

Kristina: I mean. I don't say much about myself. But if nobody else would talk, I wouldn't say *nothing*. Then she came with some ol' personal stuff and I was like "damn!" I could talk in here.

The moment to which these students alluded occurred early in October, as the class moved from the Roots of Hip-Hop and Literature unit to the Love unit. Our first reading from the unit was "Manifest" by Lauryn Hill, a first-person narrative about a bad relationship:

You see I loved hard once, but the love wasn't returned
I found out the man I'd die for, he wasn't even concerned
And time it turned
He tried to burn me like a perm
Though my eyes saw the deception, my heart wouldn't let me
learn
For um, some, dumb woman, was I,
And every time he'd lie he would cry and inside I'd die.
My heart must have died a thousand deaths
Compared myself to Toni Braxton thought I'd never catch my
breath
Nothing left, he stole the heart beating from my chest
I tried to call the cops, that type of thief you can't arrest
Pain suppressed, will lead to cardiac arrest
Diamonds deserve diamonds, but he convinced me I was
worth less
When my peoples would protest,
I told them mind their business, cause my shit was complex
More than just the sex
I was blessed, but couldn't feel like it when I was caressed
I'd spend nights clutching my breasts overwhelmed by God's
test
I was God's best contemplating death with a Gillette
But no man is ever worth the paradise manifest

After reading "Manifest," we engaged in a spirited conversation about the meaning of particular parts of the song. Like previous class sessions, there was much debate over the meaning of the last two lines of the text. While most students (along with Mr. Colombo and I) assumed that Lauryn Hill was contemplating suicide, several students emphatically argued that Hill was considering killing her lover with a razor. After debating over the meaning of the lines for a few minutes, one of the students who was vigorously advocating for the second interpretation rhetorically asked, "I mean, who would kill they *self* over somebody else?" I decided that his question provided a perfect segue for a more personal discussion of the text and responded, "That's an interesting question. Has anyone felt like Lauryn does in 'Manifest'? Not just the suicide part, either." The class suddenly grew quiet as heads began to shake left and right indicating "no." A few minutes later, class ended.

The following day, I began the class with a journal question that picked up where we had left off the previous day. The board read:

"I loved hard once but the love wasn't returned." Can you
relate to this? If so, how?

As soon as they entered the classroom, most of the students, as well as Mr. Colombo and I, sat down and wrote what appeared to be detailed responses to the question. After 15 minutes, I signaled the end of the writing period by asking, "So who wants to share?" Two full minutes of nearly complete silence passed before being interrupted by Robin's half-raised hand and soft voice.

"I do. I got a story to tell," Robin said, without moving her eyes from her notebook. Robin is a short, heavy-set Cambodian girl with big bright cheeks and a quiet demeanor. She is 23 years old and has lived on her own since she became pregnant at 16 and her parents forced her to leave home. She works full-time at a local supermarket and raises her 2-year-old biracial son without help from his father, whom she hasn't seen in 18 months. When she leans forward, the slightly undersized velour sweatsuits that she wears almost daily reveal the bottom half of a large red tattoo written across her back that reads: "LOVE HURTS." Robin is the oldest student in the class and hasn't been to school since she dropped out 7 years ago. Unable to find a steady job, she decided to return to school to obtain her diploma and continue on to college in order to better provide for her son. She doesn't say much to the other students, which gives her an air of mysteriousness that causes them to listen to her with curious attention whenever she speaks.

"I loved hard once," she said, barely above a whisper. After a deliberate but unpretentious pause she continued:

> I mean, I know exactly what she talking about. I was in love with this boy when I was young. I gave him everything. I put him above everybody including my father. Everybody told me I was trippin' but I ain't listen. I gave him everything and he didn't love me for real for real. I got pregnant and he just left. If it wasn't for my son, I don't know what I would've did to myself. I knew he needed me. Otherwise, I don't know.

Robin's personal narrative, which most of us recollect as the first one articulated within the class, represents the most important and difficult component of wounded healing: *personal disclosure*. As she later told me, her willingness to expose her wounds by sharing a personal and painful story was animated by a desire to "help somebody else through they own shit." Although there was no indication that the story that Robin shared related to another student's personal experience, it nonetheless facilitated the formation of a classroom community in which students shared their own stories and responded to others.

Robin's decision to tell her story marked a watershed moment in the Hip-Hop Lit school year, as it encouraged other students to engage in similar storytelling acts. As Kristina noted above, Robin's disclosure showed the other members of the class that they "could talk in here." Kristina's use of "could" is critical because it refers not to the students having official permission to tell their stories, as the course was explicitly designed to encourage storytelling. Rather, "could" refers to the construction of new possibilities for members of Hip-Hop Lit. By offering her story, Robin enabled the other students in Hip-Hop Lit to begin imagining the classroom as a potentially safe site for sharing their stories. After her disclosure, many students began to explore the possibilities of the classroom for storytelling by increasing the frequency, depth, and personal nature of their stories.

Like Robin's story, the most personal and engaging narratives that were shared in class typically emerged unexpectedly during normal classroom instruction. Students would insert their stories into the conversation and, after they received a response, return to their previous activity. These events typically lasted no more than a few minutes and rarely subverted the rhythm of the class despite their apparent disconnection from the formal curriculum. An example of this occurred as I was teaching a lesson on mood and tone using Tupac's "Dear Mama":

> *Me*: [S]o what is the mood of this piece?
>
> *Joe*: Sad.
>
> *Me*: Why?
>
> *Joe*: After all . . . he went through with his moms, he had to be sad.
>
> *Me*: But isn't he thanking her for being a good mom in spite of everything?
>
> *Joe*: Yeah but you gotta be sad going through that. Me and mom and my brother went through the same shit.
>
> *Jay*: Me too. More me than my brother but my pop wasn't there so shit gonna be sad. But you still happy 'cause you made it through.
>
> *Me*: I know he might've been sad thinking about everything they went through. Just like y'all probably did. But if you made it and everybody was listening to your story, how you think they would feel?
>
> *Joe*: I think they would feel better. Like "Joe went through that and became a rapper or whatever so it don't gotta turn out f-ed up."
>
> *Jay*: Exactly. Like "y'all could learn from my pain."
>
> *Me*: OK. OK. That's what mood is all about. Not so much what the writer is feeling but how might the reader feel when he [sic] reads it. So what would be a good word to describe how you might feel when you read this?
>
> *Jay*: Better.
>
> *Kenef*: Happy. Like y'all said, you might feel better knowing it ain't gotta end up all crazy.
>
> *Me*: What might be a good word for that?
>
> *Mr. Colombo*: How about hopeful?
>
> *Me*: Hopeful! That sounds good. Let's say the mood is hopeful. Now, y'all really answered this but what would you say is the tone of the piece?

From my perspective, two things were happening simultaneously during this interaction. After I solicited a response to my question about the mood of the text, Joe and Jay answered by saying that the mood was sad and offered personal stories to justify their response. For them, "Dear Mama" was sad because they had similar personal stories that they relied on to understand how Tupac was feeling; the mood was sad because they remembered being sad in their own respective experiences. Although I challenged their interpretation because I was unsatisfied with their answer, which appeared to conflate mood (the atmosphere of the narrative) and tone (the character's state of being)— Tupac's "Dear Mama" is a tribute to his mother that, despite its often disturbing content, was presumably written to invoke joy, not sadness, from the audience—the personal narratives that informed their reading of the text nonetheless provided a critical point of entry for teaching the day's lesson. Equally important, the Hip-Hop Lit classroom enabled a space for wounds to be exposed and healed through the acts of co-signing and challenging.

Co-Signing

One of the primary ways that members of the classroom community responded to personal disclosures was through the act of *co-signing*, where members of the community would provide affirmation for the person exposing a wound. Co-signing served two functions: substantiating the truth-value of the narrative and encouraging the speaker to continue. Co-signing practices included nonverbal cues (e.g., head nods, empathetic facial gestures), interjections (e.g., "Exactly!" or "Mm-hmm"), and, most importantly, complementary stories. Such narrative practices can be located within the homiletical tradition of the Black church, where call-and-response interactions are engaged by the preacher and the congregation to stimulate the listener and encourage the speaker (Holt, 1999; Smitherman, 1977). These practices are equally apparent during the act of "testifyin'," where a member of the congregation shares a personal story within the formal church service as a means by which to affirm the goodness of God (Smitherman, 1977). Within this space, personal stories are often buttressed by an additional story from another member of the church community, thereby acknowledging both the commonality and the legitimacy of the narrative.

In the above interaction, Jay co-signed Joe's narrative by offering a complementary story that articulated the commonality of their respective experiences with their fathers. While such interactions may have served a therapeutic purpose, they also served the additional (and with regard to the classroom, primary) purpose of enabling a teachable moment where we could make an effective bridge between student narratives and the curriculum. Although I could have disregarded their narratives and simply explained the differences between mood and tone, I instead attempted to validate their stories by using them as a part of the lesson. As many of the students noted, this approached yielded enormous personal and practical benefits:

> *Jay*: The stuff we be learning is interesting even if we ain't talk about hip-hop. But the fact that we get to talk about our own stories make it easier to relate to everybody.
> *Robin*: Plus, sometimes in school stuff can get boring and you don't even try to understand it. When you be connecting it to our lives it's easier to follow and better to understand.
> *Dorene*: Exactly. I learn stuff easier when I could relate to it. Plus, when you get to know everybody better, with their stories and everything, it's easier to relax and pay attention.

As the students' comments suggest, it was these acts of individual disclosure and our collective response to them—both of which occurred on a daily basis—that enabled the construction of the classroom community and served as a suitable hook for sustaining student interest.

Challenging

In addition to co-signing, students often responded to personal disclosures through the act of challenging. Unlike co-signing, which was a common response to all types of stories, challenging only occurred when members of Hip-Hop Lit exposed wounds that were explicitly ideological. In my use of the term "ideological wounds," I am not alluding (as do many critical pedagogues [Ellsworth, 1989]) to "false consciousness," or a dogmatic neo-Marxian belief that the students' conceptions of the world were "damaged" by their personal experiences and therefore in need of repair. Rather, many of the beliefs about the world that were articulated within Hip-Hop Lit were largely shaped by painful encounters with forces of inequality and marginalization that had not been previously articulated or critically examined. The conversations that emerged from these ideological narratives were therefore not less personal but less *personalized*, as the entire class was able to use a particular narrative to challenge individual and collective worldviews within a relatively safe space.

Like co-signing, challenging took both verbal and nonverbal forms, the most significant being the offering of a competing narrative. Unlike personal wounds, the exposure of ideological wounds frequently led to longer, more inclusive conversations that took the class away from the planned lesson. Although the conversations that emerged from challenging were often intense, they rarely became antagonistic. The following example of this type of conversation came on the day that we read "Project Window" by Nas as part of a lesson about imagery. After discussing Nas's use of imagery in his description of the Queensbridge Housing Projects, I initiated a conversation about the relationship between "Project Window" and the students' ideas about neighborhoods:

> *Me*: So how does the imagery that Nas uses connect to your own ideas about neighborhoods?
> *Kia*: It reminded me about how neighborhoods turn into "hoods."
> *Me*: What do you mean?
> *Kia*: Black people don't know how to keep they neighborhoods. Look at where we live. Everytime I come outside people be selling drugs and they be shooting all the time. The same stuff that Nas talkin' about.
> *Dorene*: Exactly. White people keep they house clean on the outside. Black people throw stuff everywhere. That's why the hood look like it do. It don't be crackheads and stuff around White people neighborhoods.
> *Maggie*: Shiiiit. That ain't true. It's crackheads and trash and stuff in my neighborhood too!
> *Kia*: But it's different though. Y'all got silver spoons in y'all mouths. Y'all dads got companies that y'all can work at and we gotta start from the bottom. It's different when you don't got money.
> *Maggie*: I ain't got no money!
> *Lisa* [White]: Me neither. . . . Plus, I live two blocks from y'all!

This interaction represents a frequent occurrence when students explicitly linked their ideological positions to personal disclosures. In this instance, Kia explained that her conception of the Black neighborhood was informed by her experiences within her own neighborhood. Dorene co-signed the story by explaining the relationship between race and the quality of neighborhoods. Maggie then pushed the conversation into a different direction by challenging Kia with a competing story from her vantage point as a White student.

For Maggie, the students' romantic conception of White neighborhoods contradicted her own experiences as a White person living under circumstances similar to those of Dorene and Kia. Lisa co-signed Maggie's challenge by pointing out that all of the students in the conversation lived in the same neighborhood, thereby complicating Dorene and Kia's arguments about the relationship between racial identity and class position. As was usually the case, this exchange quickly ended and we returned to our formal lesson. Nevertheless, the ideas discussed became reference points for further conversations, as the students, Mr. Colombo, and I would use future class conversations and course texts to co-sign or challenge earlier claims. Through this practice, students would engage in closer readings of the texts, as well as sustained analyses of the issues raised in class.

Healing

Through the acts of personal disclosure, co-signing, and challenging, members of Hip-Hop Lit were able to engage in processes of healing. It is worth reiterating, however, that my use of "healing" neither presumes nor suggests a completed medical, psychological, or ideological recovery. Rather, it refers to the process by which members of Hip-Hop Lit were able to find varying levels of insight, relief, support, empathy, and critique within the Hip-Hop Lit community for their personal and ideological wounds.

For many students, the process of healing was primarily linked to the act of personal disclosure. Although they benefited from the community's response to their narratives, students in Hip-Hop Lit often mentioned how important it was to offer their stories in full public view, regardless of the particular response that they received. This sentiment was captured by Robin, who remarked, "Even though people say good stuff to each other, sometime it just feel good to say stuff out loud." Other students in the class offered a similar perspective about the importance of "saying stuff out loud":

Lisa: When you tell a story in front of everybody, sometimes it
feel good just to get it off your chest.

Dorene: Me too! Sometimes I don't even need nobody to say
nothing. I just need get something off my chest. Like the
time I was talking about all the drama with my baby father.
Just talkin' about how he hurt me made me feel better
because I never said it out loud before.

Although the benefits of public disclosure did not always hinge upon
the community's response, the relative safety of the classroom space
was nonetheless crucial for enabling such disclosures. In an interview, Lisa and Dorene explained the importance of the classroom
community:

Me: Now that you know how good it feels to get stuff of your
chest, do you find yourself doing it more often?

Lisa: Yes and no. I be trying but it's hard because even though
it feel good just to say it sometimes, you can't just say it
anywhere. I can say it in here cause I know everybody and
that's how we get down.

Dorene: Exactly. Even if don't nobody say nothing, you gotta
know that if you *need* some support or whatever, somebody
gon' be there. Plus you gotta know people ain't gonna tell
all your business.

Lisa: Plus I don't be thinkin' about this stuff until we be readin'.

The observations of Lisa and Dorene underscore the importance of the
Hip-Hop Lit community in facilitating the healing process. Even when
people found healing primarily through the act of disclosure, Hip-Hop
Lit served as a relatively safe space in which people felt that their disclosures could be heard, responded to, and protected. Also, the narratives within the course texts often connected to students' experiences
in ways that created organic opportunities for disclosure.

While many students found relief in personal disclosures, most
students, including those mentioned above, often spoke about the
value of engaging with the stories of their classmates. In the case
of Joe and Jay, understanding the commonality of their experiences
with their fathers was a critical part of their healing process. As Joe
explained:

It just feel good sometimes to hear that other people is goin'
through the same shit. Me and Jay not even that cool. I mean
we don't got beef or nothin' but I don't know him like that. . . .
But he still was like "I been through the same bullshit with my
pops." That shit is so real because sometimes you be like "Why
this had to happen to me?" Then you realize that it happens to
everybody.

In a separate conversation, Jay added:

It's crazy cause you might not even know somebody but you
could still feel they pain. You don't be *happy* 'cause they goin'
through it but it feel good to know it's not just you.

For Joe and Jay, the usefulness of their interaction rested upon its ability to expose the commonality of their experiences.

In addition to providing personal pleasure for students, the process of healing also informed students' performance of classroom
assignments. For example, Joe and Jay used class assignments to negotiate their issues with their absentee fathers. As part of a creative
writing assignment in our "despair" unit, Jay and Joe began to work
collaboratively on a rap about a young boy in the ghetto who con-
templates suicide after finding out that his "deadbeat" father lived
around the corner from him but did not want to meet him. Other students, such as Robin, Dorene, and Lisa, frequently used their journal
assignments to write about abusive relationships. At the end of the
semester, they spoke about the importance of class activities for the
healing process:

Lisa: Even though we were learning literature and writing, we
    also got to deal with personal stuff. By the end of the year I
    felt a lot better.
Dorene: Yeah, like every time we wrote about our triflin'
    boyfriends, I learned how to avoid [them] in the future.
Lisa: Plus we got cool with each other because we was all in the
    same boat!
Dorene: Yeah, 'cause I used to think it was all my fault. By the
    end it was all good.

In a separate interview, Joe expressed a similar feeling:

When Jay and I made that song about the kid who lost his pop, we got real cool. Before that, we didn't really know each other but after that we became like family. It was mad cool to learn that everybody has struggles and, by the end of the class, I wasn't as mad anymore. Don't get me wrong, I'm not over it but I'm dealing better.

Although some of the students may have overstated the transformative effects of the class, their remarks nonetheless speak to the possibilities of Hip-Hop Lit for enabling the healing process.

FORMATION OF COMMUNITY

As wounded healing became a common occurrence, the classroom community began to take a unique shape. The bounds of the community were established and policed in tacit, varied, and often complicated ways. Although they were not always explicitly articulated, multiple designations were used to assess and respond to an individual's status within the community. It was through these designations, and the practices undergirding them, that the classroom community was formed. Through the roles outlined in this section we are able to understand how the practices of wounded healing within Hip-Hop Lit positioned the various members of the community.

Regulars

Within the class was a group of 11 students, the regulars, who formed the core of the community. Mr. Colombo and I depended on regulars to speak when there were lulls in conversation or no one seemed willing to answer questions that we deemed important. Other students also relied upon regulars to answer questions about class assignments and to be the first to respond to questions posed by Mr. Colombo and me. While most of the regulars attended class daily, the primary criterion for being a regular was not attendance but participation in classroom conversations. For example, Anita, an Indian student who did not speak English fluently and rarely engaged in classroom conversation, was not considered a regular despite her daily attendance. Conversely, Shaheem, who almost never attended class more than twice a week but frequently participated, was considered a regular by the students and me. Although there were days on which regulars elected not to participate, such moments were extremely rare.

Regulars understood their role, and many took pride in Mr. Colombo's and my dependency on them. When called on, they would often feign annoyance and demand to know why they were always "picked on" to answer questions. Privately, however, many intimated that they enjoyed the attention and respect of being considered regulars. Robin, who quickly became a regular, offered:

> It don't really bother me that y'all be calling on me all the time. Sometime I don't feel like talking but I know you need me! [laughs] Plus, it ain't no other class where we get treated like we important because we got a story or something happened to us.

In addition to recognizing their own role, regulars used their position as classroom leaders to explicitly define or tacitly identify many of the other roles that emerged within the community.

Outsiders

The boundaries of the class were most apparent when outsiders, those people who were not an official part of the class, approached or traversed them. The presence of outside students, teachers, and administrators almost always disturbed the rhythm of the class and disenabled many classroom conversations. Mr. Ormond once joked: "Damn, Marc, it's like you're running a cult in here. If I come in to look for a student or pick up attendance, everybody stops and looks at me like I'm crazy."

Mr. Ormond's remark alludes to the students' tendency to stop talking or change the conversation when outsiders entered the classroom. He made the comment after walking into the classroom during a conversation about relationships and love that emerged from reading "Ms. Jackson" by Outkast. Shaheem, a regular, had just begun to speak about his own experiences with his girlfriend. Although Shaheem was a regular, he rarely commented on topics that compromised the hypermasculine stance that he and his friends frequently assumed in class. On this day, however, Shaheem began to explain how Outkast member Andre 3000's use of imagery ("together dream about that crib with the Goodyear swing") reminded him of his own experience with his girlfriend and how they envisioned a life together before "things went downhill."

As he began his next sentence ("Love is crazy 'cause . . ."), Mr. Ormond walked in and quietly whispered something to Mr. Colombo. The moment that Mr. Ormond entered the room, Shaheem stopped talking. Intrigued by his vulnerability and interested in his comments, I encouraged Shaheem to finish. He replied that he had "forgot what I was gonna say." After Mr. Ormond closed the door behind him, Shaheem smiled coyly and shouted, "Oh yeah! I remember" and then continued to share. Such occurrences were common, as the presence of outsiders immediately affected the content and quality of classroom conversation.

Some of the students indicated that they did this because they felt, despite Mr. Colombo's and my frequent assurances to the contrary, that many of our conversations were inappropriate for school and could jeopardize the status of the class and our jobs. Most of the students, however, expressed reluctance to share or comment on personal stories in front of people who were not a part of the class, even those with whom they had close out-of-class relationships.

For example, Stanley, a student from another class, would come into Hip-Hop Lit for a few minutes daily to speak to Jay, his best friend, who was also a regular in Hip-Hop Lit. One day during the middle of the year, I noticed that I hadn't seen Stanley in over a month and I asked Jay why he had stopped coming to school. He told me that Stanley still attended every day, but no longer came into the class. I asked Jay why, genuinely assuring him that I had no problem with their daily interaction. Jay responded that he did not want to "disrespect the class" by having an outsider enter the class. He then pointed out that he would request a hall pass every day and leave Hip-Hop Lit to visit Stanley in his class, where "they don't do nothin' anyway." Jay's decision reflected the sentiment of many regulars that, unlike other classes, Hip-Hop Lit was a community that needed and deserved protection from nonmembers.

Extras

In addition to the core number of students in Hip-Hop Lit who came to class frequently, there was a group of four or five students who attended class sporadically. Mr. Colombo labeled these students "extras," in reference to the insignificant (and typically nonspeaking) characters in a movie or television show. These students worked diligently when they came to class but often disappeared for several weeks at a time. Many of the extras were not interested in completing the program and only came to school to socialize with friends, buy or use marijuana and alcohol in the bathrooms, or satisfy the minimal conditions of their parole or probation by remaining on the active attendance roll. While a few extras gained interest in the course and became regulars—Shaheem, for example, began the school year as an extra and became a regular—most remained on the periphery of the class for the entire school year.

Because of their poor attendance, extras devoted most of their time to answering old journal questions and completing late classwork. Although they would respond to questions about the course texts, extras rarely offered personal stories and only occasionally commented on the stories of other members of the class. Kwame, one of the extras, explained:

> I know I don't come all the time so when I do, I don't wanna
> wreck y'all flow, y'ah mean? Y'all be talking about shit and
> I feel like I'm in *y'all business* so I just fall back and listen . . .
> [laughing] I don't really say much about myself 'cause I don't
> know y'all like that [emphasis added].

Kwame's feeling of being an outsider was reinforced by many of the regulars. An example of this came during a classroom conversation in which Ryan, another extra, attempted to participate in a conversation that the students were having about a story that a student had shared. Keneka, one of the regulars, turned to him and matter-of-factly said, "Mind your business!" Keneka's comment reflected the general sentiment that extras were members of the class (which distinguished them from outsiders), but not of the wounded healing community.

Listeners

Unlike extras and outsiders, listeners were the four or five official members of the class who attended regularly but rarely participated in classroom conversations that involved personal disclosure. Some of the listeners were students like Anita, who attended daily but did not feel that they had anything to contribute to the class. While Anita's reluctance was due in part to language difficulty, students like Michelle felt that their stories simply were not worth sharing:

> Everybody be having deep stories and everything. I don't be having nothing to say except dumb shit so I just listen.

As this quote suggests, many of the listeners did not feel that their stories were legitimate for inclusion within the classroom. The belief that their stories weren't sufficiently "deep" prevented many students like Anita from participating in classroom conversation.

Other listeners, like Alisha, did not question the legitimacy of their stories but were uncomfortable offering their stories in front of the class:

> I don't want to say nothing in class because I'm a private person. It's not that I don't want to participate. Like [long pause] I do the work and everything but I don't want to talk about stuff.

Regardless of their reasons for not participating, listeners usually demonstrated their engagement with the course through their journals. A typical example of this came as the students offered their journal responses to the question, "Have you or any one you know ever considered suicide? What did you/they do?" Due to the sensitive nature of the question, we made sharing with the rest of the class optional. Nevertheless, as was almost always the case, nearly every student responded to the question as we went around the discussion circle. Alisha and Michelle, however, both insisted that they did not have a problem with sharing but had nothing to say about the topic. After class, I read both of their responses:

> *Alisha*: One time, me and my boyfriend broke up and I felt like I couldn't live without him. I wasn't really going to do nothing but you still think about it.
> *Michelle*: I think everybody has thought about suicide at one time or another. Sometime things don't go the way you want them to and you are going to wonder if its worth it.

As their journal entries demonstrate, both Alisha and Michelle were capable of sharing stories that were relevant to the question and sufficiently personal. Further, as listeners they were able to engage in wounded healing by sharing their stories through their journals while observing and partially participating in classroom healing practices. The fact that they shared their stories with no one other than Mr. Colombo and me, however, created tensions between the listeners and the regulars.

Toward the middle of the year, as it became more apparent who was willing to speak, many regulars began to express their wariness of the listeners. As Dorene intimated to me in an after-class conversation:

> Sometime I don't want to say shit because it be people in here that don't never say nothin'. It make you not wanna talk cause you not sure you could trust them. It's like when you got a girlfriend that you tell all your business to but she don't say none of hers. It make them seem shady, like "Who they telling my business to?"

While Dorene's sentiments were not uncommon, they contradicted the listeners' explanations of how they responded to personal narratives in class. In response to a journal question, Michelle wrote:

> I don't say a lot when people tell there stories but I listen and learn a lot. It feels good to hear that other people think the same way about stuff. Sometime I want to say something because I don't agree with everything but I don't. Still, I learned a whole lot.

Part of the regulars' misinterpretation of the listeners' motives was due to the fact that no one but Mr. Colombo and I knew the degree to which students like Michelle were engaging in and responding to storytelling through their journals. Although I would often say things to the class like, "Some of you write very interesting things in your journal but never speak in class," in order to make it clear that the listeners weren't merely eavesdropping on the regulars, our decision not to share the specifics of the listeners' written responses undermined our attempts at eliminating some of the tensions.

Despite skepticism from many of the regulars, listeners were nonetheless met with a level of empathy and openness that was not reserved for outsiders and extras. While extras were often rejected when they attempted to share advice or draw from their personal experiences, listeners were frequently encouraged to contribute to the class conversations. Mr. Colombo noted, "I think when kids like Michelle don't talk it's different than other kids. It's like, everybody knows she's trying." For example, during a conversation about drugs, I asked how many people in the class had smoked "weed" (marijuana). Michelle, whose hand was one of the many that were raised, added, "But I don't no more." Keneka responded half-playfully and half-authoritatively, "Why not? Now I *know* you got a story about weed 'cause you smiling and you raised your hand." Although we were clearly veering away from our primary conversation, I encouraged Michelle to comply with Keneka's request. When Michelle declined, a look of disappointment appeared on the faces of Keneka and several other members of the class, including me. In addition to missing out on a potentially interesting story, at least a few of us were more disappointed that Michelle squandered an opportunity to move more closely to the center of the community.

TEACHING (AS) WOUNDED HEALERS (OR NOT)

As indicated in the previous section, many roles developed in the classroom community in relationship to the practices of wounded healing. With respect to Mr. Colombo and me, these roles were further complicated by the teacher–student power relationships within the class. Despite our common position as co-teachers, each of us responded to our position within the storytelling community in drastically different ways.

My position within Hip-Hop Lit underwent dramatic shifts throughout the year. Like many of the students, I was extremely apprehensive at the beginning of the semester about sharing my personal stories in full public view. As such, my primary role at the beginning of the year was that of a listener. Because of my position as a teacher, I was often favorably positioned in a relationship of *one-sided storytelling*, where a person or group offers personal narratives as the other person or group is empowered to listen, judge, and respond based on their assessment of the narrative. In the case of Hip-Hop Lit, the students would tell their personal stories while Mr. Colombo and I listened and responded.

Like in most urban schools, one-sided storytelling extended beyond the bounds of the formal curriculum and into other, "hidden" dimensions of the classroom. For example, early in the year Robin approached me and told me that the reason that she had been absent the previous day was because she could not find child care. She told me that she could not afford her usual babysitter because she did not have enough money and her son's father was not providing financial support. Although she did not have to provide as much personal detail as she did, the program's allegedly strict attendance policy forced students to provide "an *acceptable* excuse for all absences" (Twilight Program Memo, emphasis added). By positioning teachers and administrators as arbiters of acceptability, students who were unable to attend class or stay for the entire period because of court appearances, child care issues, or other personal problems were forced to disclose these deeply personal parts of their lives to relative strangers who offered judgment (approval, dismissal, etc.) in exchange.

The one-sided nature of this relationship first became apparent to me in mid-October when I entered the class wearing a "North Philly" t-shirt. One of the students immediately said to me, "What you doin' with a N.P. shirt on?" I explained to their amazement that "I was born on Luzerne Street," a well-known street in North Philadelphia. Up to that point, the students did not know that I was born and partly raised in North Philadelphia, even though I knew the neighborhoods, streets, and often the houses in which they lived. Such events were extremely common in Hip-Hop Lit, just as they are in other traditional and nontraditional educational settings, where students are explicitly or implicitly coerced into exposing their personal selves while teachers and other authority figures are empowered to decide which stories they want to reveal.

The practice of one-sided storytelling was equally evident though far more complicated as Mr. Colombo and I began to teach Hip-Hop Lit. As students wrote in their daily journals, Mr. Colombo and I (per our agreement with the class) would respond to the question of the day in our own journals. Although we responded to each question— at times, however, teaching demands allowed us only enough time to give an oral response—our early responses were, like those of the rest of the class, relatively impersonal. By the time the Love unit began, however, my responses had become increasingly personal. During that unit, in response to the question "I loved hard once . . . ," I read the following response from my journal after Robin shared hers:

> I loved a girl once when I lived in Atlanta for college. We were friends since I was seventeen and I fell in love with her,

although I didn't realize it until later. She loved me as a friend
but not in a romantic way. I never told her how I felt until I saw
her . . . the summer before last. She gave me the impression
that we had a chance but when I got home she fronted on me. I
was sick about that for a minute.

Disclosures like this one became common for me within the class. Despite their personal veneer, however, these stories required little effort
for me to share. It was not until later in the year that I became comfortable enough to share the stories in which I had a personal, emotional
investment and a genuine need for healing. One of the first occasions
occurred as we began the Family unit.

During that unit we read "Ms. Jackson" by Outkast, in which Big
Boi and Andre 3000 (the group's members) write letters to Ms. Jackson, the fictional grandmother (what they call the "baby's momma's
momma") of their children. We began a discussion of Andre 3000's use
of imagery in the second verse of the song:

Ten times out of nine
Now if I'm lyin', fine
The quickest muzzle throw it on my mouth and I'll decline
King meets queen, then the puppy love thing, together dream
'Bout that crib with the Goodyear swing
On the oak tree, I hope we feel like this forever
Forever, forever, ever? Forever, ever?
Forever never seem that long until you're grown
And notice that the day-by-day ruler can't be too wrong
Ms. Jackson my intentions were good I wish I could
Become a magician to abracadabra all the sadder
Thoughts of me, thoughts of she, thoughts of he
Askin' what happened to the feelin' that her and me
Had, I pray so much about it need some knee, pads
It happened for a reason one can't be, mad
So know this, know that everything's cool
And yes I will be present on the first day of school, and
     graduation

We performed a text rendering of the song and many of the students
focused on the line "Forever, forever, ever. Forever, ever?" and others, including me, recognized "Forever never seem that long until

you're grown" as the line that stood out to them. I asked the students to talk about why those two lines were so significant, and several of them responded with stories about relationships that they thought would last forever but abruptly ended. While I nodded with approval as the students told their stories, Dorene stared at me quizzically before finally asking, "What *you* know about this, Mr. Hill?" I fought the urge to ignore or playfully dismiss her question, as I had often done up to that point when faced with a personal question. Instead, I responded:

> That line, "Forever never seem that long until you're grown" is deep to me. I mean, I'm thinking about the song and how I can feel that in my own life. I have a baby on the way right now that I didn't expect. Her mom is six months pregnant and I'm really stressin' about it. I ain't worried about money or nothin' like that. It's just . . . I wasn't expecting this and she and I not together and she [the mother] gotta be in my life forever. So I'm like "*Forever*, ever? *Forever* ever?" That's a long-ass time! [class laughs] This just wasn't how I thought about it back when I was a kid. I thought I'd end up married to the person that I have kids with and even when she told me she was pregnant the thought crossed my mind to just get married but I knew that wasn't right because we would've been miserable.

The class suddenly grew quiet as the students and Mr. Colombo stared at me to see if I was done sharing. When they seemed confident that I was, they began to respond:

> *Hakeem*: I feel you. Baby moms be trippin'.
> *Kanef*: You should know! All them kids you got!!
> *Hakeem*: Shut up! I'm serious. [Mr. Hill], I went through the same. . . . I thought I was gonna be wit' my baby mom and then [it] got crazy.
> *Me*: It's not that I wanted to be with her. It just crossed my mind. . . .
> *Dorene*: That's 'cause everybody act like it's what you supposed to do but you gotta do what's best for you. It's like the song say, forever is a long time.
> *Me*: Yeah you right. "Forever never seem that long until you're grown."

Hakeem: You just gotta make sure that she don't get mad . . .
   about money or 'cause you not messin' with her and not let
   you see the kids.
Me: [looking at the entire class] I feel you. Based on what we've
   read, how do you y'all think Andre and Big Boi feel about
   their situations?

This brief interaction, which I deliberately ended by posing a question about the text, is significant because it was the first time that I exposed my own wounds in front of the students. After class I wrote:

I told the students about my situation with the baby. I was
surprised at how thoughtful and helpful they were when they
heard about my story. Even more surprising to me is how much
better I felt about the situation after talking to them. Although
they didn't tell me anything that I didn't already know, there
was something special about sharing that particular experience
with my students.

Hakeem, who was 17 years old with two children born 1 month apart, and Dorene, who was 18 years old with a 6-month-old baby, both listened to my story and responded with advice that was thoughtful, helpful, and informed by their own personal experiences. For the first time, I felt like I was not in complete control of the class as a teacher, but another member of the storytelling community. Although my power to end the conversation when I deemed it appropriate affirms that I never completely ceded my authority as teacher, there was nonetheless a moment in class when I felt as if my story was no more or less important than the others.

According to Keneka, one of the most engaged regulars in Hip-Hop Lit, it was this type of practice that strengthened the bond between the students and me. She told me that the "only reason how you . . . get with us is because you be tellin' us your lifetime stories. You don't lie. You keep it real." As Keneka's quote suggests, it was not only my willingness to expose my wounds, but the coherence of my particular wounds with their own that helped legitimate my status within the community. To many of the students in Hip-Hop Lit, my life was real enough to warrant entry into the community.

Mr. Colombo, however, experienced great difficulty joining the community of wounded healers. Like several of the students, Mr. Colombo was extremely uncomfortable sharing his stories in class. He also saw his position as teacher as prohibitive with regard to storytelling. After the students left class on the day that I told the students my story about the baby, Mr. Colombo said to me, "Wow. You told them a *lot.*" I asked if he could share such a personal story and he replied, "I mean, I don't mind telling them stuff but some stuff I think teachers shouldn't tell students. You want them to see you in a certain way and they're lookin' for stuff to use against you." As Mr. Colombo was telling me this, I felt as if he were both explaining his own stance and subtly offering advice that he hoped would dissuade me from further such disclosures.

Mr. Colombo's position on personal disclosure quickly became apparent to the students as the school year persisted. While students who were designated as listeners were met with a mix of empathy and wariness, Mr. Colombo's silence was uniformly rejected by the students, who would frequently request that he share "real" stories. By the middle of the year, the students' disdain for Mr. Colombo's reticence was reflected in their interactions with him. For example, when Mr. Colombo would ask a question, Dorene, a regular, and Angel, an extra, would mockingly ask (in a caricaturesque Middle American White male voice), "How do *you* feel about this, Colombo? What does this remind *you* of?" Mr. Colombo would typically respond by laughing and changing the subject or saying, "I'm more interested in what *you* guys think."

One day, when Mr. Colombo did not come to school and I was teaching the class by myself, Dorene sparked the following conversation:

Dorene: How come Mr. Colombo don't never tell us nothing?
Me: What do you mean?
Dorene: You know what I'm talkin' about, [Mr. Hill]. You be talkin' and telling us stuff but if you ask him something he don't wanna say nothin'.
Keneka: I know! He act like he too good to talk.
Me: I don't think it's that. . . . Maybe he's just not comfortable yet.
Keneka: How you gonna ask us to do all this talkin' and [in a mocking voice] "sharing our feelings" and you don't say nothing. That shit is corny.
Josh: I don't he think he do it on purpose. He just, y'ah mean, he can't relate 'cause he's from, you know, a different culture so he don't want to say nothin'.

Dorene: N'aah. Other people can't relate too but they try
[pauses]. And he a *teacher*.

As Dorene pointed out, Mr. Colombo's position as teacher created a different set of expectations with regard to his participation. While other listeners were excused for their lack of participation or at worst viewed skeptically, Mr. Colombo was expected to offer more of himself due to his extraordinary access to students' stories and his perceived power in relation to the students.

Despite his refusal to offer personal narratives, Mr. Colombo did not express any dissonance about listening to other students' stories. In fact, hearing student stories was a critical part of the agenda that largely informed our curriculum development process. Nevertheless, Mr. Colombo was at his quietest when students offered their own stories. Typically, Mr. Colombo would listen as students shared their ideas, beliefs, and personal stories and offer little in response except for a perfunctory nod of his head or an empathetic "thank you." He rarely discussed student stories within our curriculum meetings, and he admittedly did not attempt to let the stories inform his teaching. He told me:

> I feel like we're helping the kids by listening to them. I'm guessing that a lot of the stuff that they tell us they don't get to tell anybody else. And to be honest, I think it's interesting what they're telling us. I'm learning a lot about kids . . . not just the kids in class but other kids like them.

As his comment suggests, Mr. Colombo was often positioned within the class as a voyeur who engaged in one-sided storytelling for the purpose of what Foucault (1990) calls "the pleasure of analysis," or a self-centered obsession with the sources of pleasure (or in this case pain) of another person. It was this type of surveillance, or at least its perception, that further marginalized Mr. Colombo within the class.

The relationship among Mr. Colombo, me, and the rest of the Hip-Hop Lit community with regard to storytelling is critical for understanding the power dynamics of the class. Although teachers can never relinquish classroom power (Gore, 1998; O'Reilly, 1993), the willingness to render oneself vulnerable can reorganize classroom power relations in ways that allow for more democratic, engaged, and productive practices. Such a gesture is particularly important in spaces like Hip-Hop Lit, where students are being asked to confess desires, share secrets, or otherwise offer aspects of themselves that have been traditionally excluded from the formal schooling process. By contrast, the failure to do so can further marginalize and silence both students and teachers in ways that undermine the spirit of wounded healing.

OPEN(ING) WOUNDS: ACTS OF SILENCING AND HURTING

Despite the collective success of Hip-Hop Lit in creating a community of wounded healers, there were clear tensions that appeared as the conversations became more personal. Due to the high level of intimacy within the community, members occasionally took the liberty of asking questions and telling stories that were potentially uncomfortable to others. When it became clear that a question was "too much" for someone, Mr. Colombo and I (and sometimes other regulars within the class) would redirect the conversation to another person or topic. The success of our attempts, however, was dependent on the students' ability and desire to expose their discomfort and our ability to respond effectively. What we often failed to do, however, was listen to the silences and acts of silencing (Fine, 1991; Schultz, 2003) that our conversations created. The most memorable example of this came through the following vignette. Although it represents the most extreme instance, the vignette nonetheless serves as a telling case that illustrates some of the fundamental tensions and problems that developed within the Hip-Hop Lit community.

As was our daily practice, I sent the day's journal question as a cellular text message to Mr. Colombo as I rushed to Howard High so that the students could begin writing before I arrived. We were beginning the second section of our unit on family, which dealt with abortion, and I did not want my tardiness to cause us to lose any discussion time for what I expected to be a very spirited and engaged conversation. No sooner had I walked through the classroom door than I heard the voice of Keneka, who demanded that I tell her why I had chosen the day's journal question.

Keneka was a tall 18-year-old African American girl whose bright smile often betrayed the tough front that she offered her classmates and teachers. Before returning to graduate school, I had been Keneka's Spanish teacher during day school, and I also had been her summer school Spanish teacher for the past two summers. During that time Keneka and I had developed a playfully antagonistic relationship that, to the uninitiated, would look like blatant and mutual disrespect. In front of other people, she and I would argue, tease each other, and even feign irritation at the sound of the other's voice. Mr. Colombo once remarked that he had never seen two people, much less a student and teacher, interact with each other the way Keneka and I did. His remark, which seemed to reflect the attitude of most of our audiences, did not matter to us. Our relationship was an unspoken inside joke that only we shared, and it was my understanding of our relationship that mediated my interactions with her on this day.

I responded to Keneka by joking that Mr. Colombo had picked the question and that I was as surprised as she was at the nature of the question. Unfazed by my attempts at humor, she sternly replied, "No he didn't. He already showed us the text [message] you had sent him. Why did *you* pick *that*??!!!" She then pointed to the day's question and read each word with such disgust that it seemed as if she could taste the words: "Do you believe in abortion? Explain. If you have a story, please share." As I scrambled to think of an appropriate response to Keneka's question, I looked around the room and noticed that several students, all female, were not writing anything. Since the students were frequently resistant to journal writing, I dismissed their inactivity as coincidental and decided that Keneka's concerns were not reflective of the rest of the class. I also assumed that Keneka was not angry, but merely upping the stakes in our daily game of the verbal sparring.

After the students finished writing in their journals, I asked them to share their responses. One by one, each student answered the question and provided an explanation for why they believed in or disapproved of abortion. When I got to Keneka, the following exchange occurred:

Me: What do you think?
Keneka: Yeah.
Me: What do you mean, "Yeah"???
Keneka: Yeah!!!!!!

As was our daily ritual, Keneka gave a one-word answer to a question ("Do you believe in abortion?") for which I clearly wanted and asked for a detailed response. Normally, after a bit of prodding, Keneka would follow with a long and thoughtful response to the day's question. This time, however, she closed her book and turned to the person next to her, signifying that she was done participating in the activity. I decided not to push her further and moved on to the next student.

After the rest of the students read their entries, Mr. Colombo distributed our reading for the day, "Retrospect for Life" by Common. Through text rendering, we read the entire piece:

> Knowin' you the best part of life, do I have the right to take
>   yours
> 'Cause I created you, irresponsibly
> Subconsciously, knowin' the act I was a part of
> The start of somethin', I'm not ready to bring into the world
> Had myself believin' I was thorough
> I look into mother's stomach, wonder if you are a boy or a girl
> Turnin' this woman's womb into a tomb
> But she and I agreed, a seed we don't need
> You would've been much more than a mouth to feed
> But someone, I woulda fed this information I read
> To someone, my life for you I woulda had to lead
> Instead I led you to death
> I'm sorry for takin' your first breath, first step, and first cry
> But I wasn't prepared mentally nor financially
> Havin' a child shouldn't have to bring out the man in me
> Plus I wanted you to be raised within a family
> I don't wanna, go through the drama of havin' a baby's
>   momma
> Weekend visits and buyin' J's ain't gon' make me a father
> For a while bearing a child is somethin' I never wanted to do
> For me to live forever I can only do that through you
> Nerve I got to talk about them niggaz with a gun
> Must have really thought I was God to take the life of my son
> I could have sacrificed goin' out
> To think my homies who did it I used to joke about, from now
>   on
> I'ma use self control instead of birth control
> Cause $315 ain't worth your soul
> $315 ain't worth your soul
> $315 ain't worth it
>
> Seeing you as a present and a gift in itself
> You had our child in you, I probably never feel what you felt

But you dealt with it like the strong Black woman you are
Through our trials and tribulations, child's elimination
An integration of thoughts I feel about the situation
Back and forth my feelings was pacin'
Happy deep down but not joyed enough to have it
But even that's a lie, in less than two weeks, we was back at it
Is this unprotected love or safe to say it's lust
Bustin', more than a sweat in somebody you trust
Or is it that we don't trust each other enough
And believe, havin' this child'll make us have to stay together
Girl I want you in my life cause you have made it better
Thinkin' we all in love cause we can spend a day together
We talkin' spendin' the rest of our lives
It's too many Black women that can say they mothers
But can't say that they wives
I wouldn't chose any other to mother my understanding
But I want our parenthood to come from planning
It's so much in my life that's undone
We gotta see eye to eye, about family, before we can become
  one
If you had decided to have it the situation I wouldn't run from
But I'm walkin', findin' myself and my God
So I can, discipline my son with my Rod
Not have a judge tellin' me how and when to raise my seed
Though his death was at our greed, with no one else to blame
I had a book of African names, case our minds changed
You say your period hasn't came, and lately I've been sleepy
So quit smokin' the weed and the beadies and let's have this
  boy

After doing a text rendering of "Retrospect for Life," I attempted to start a class discussion about the song by posing several questions: "Who is Common addressing in this text?" "What is the tone of the piece?" "What did Common mean by 'Three hundred and fifteen dollars ain't worth your soul?" Instead of the normal blend of waving hands and competing voices, I was met with a curious silence that intensified as my questions persisted. Determined to keep the class moving, I began to look for regulars to call on to answer my questions. As my eyes scanned the room, students' heads and bodies began to turn in order to avoid making eye contact with me.

Finally, after several long minutes passed with little progress, I wondered out loud, "How come y'all not answering the questions?" Keneka, who had been slumped in her seat and seemingly inattentive, jumped to attention as if she had been waiting all day for the question. Without hesitation, she said, "Because they didn't like the song!" Although slightly relieved that she was paying attention, I was more annoyed by the confidence with which she spoke for the entire class. "Retrospect for Life" was one of my favorite songs and its discussion of a regretted abortion seemed extremely provocative. I was convinced that either Keneka was having a bad day and being belligerent (which was not uncommon for her), or that she was simply mistaken about the class's opinion. Determined to prove that she was in the minority, I responded to her comment:

> *Me*: Well, don't speak for everybody. But why don't *you* like the
>   song?
> *Keneka*: Because I didn't.
> *Me*: I need a more elaborate response to than that. We're in a . . .
> *Keneka*: [much louder and seemingly annoyed] Because I *didn't*!

I was now sure that Keneka was merely being oppositional and had no desire to be a productive participant in the class. Although I was growing increasingly frustrated and mildly angry at her now not-so-cute resistance, I was equally determined not to let the other students see me lose my composure:

> *Me*: (in a low voice) I understand that you don't like it, but I
>   need your help in explaining to me why the text was bad so
>   that we don't got to read other stuff like this in the future.
> *Keneka*: Don't pick stuff like *this* anymore!
> *Me*: What is it about *this* that I should consider when picking a
>   song?

At this point Haneef, a student who rarely came to class and spoke even less, was unable to tolerate my ignorance any further and exclaimed, "She don't like it because it's about abortion." Without missing a beat, Keneka added, "Basically!" to punctuate Haneef's declaration of the apparently obvious.

Finally, I had managed to feel as dumb as I must have looked to my students. A sick feeling came over me as I stumbled through the remainder of the class, speaking vaguely about tone and mood while attempting to find meaning in Keneka's distant expression. Although Keneka and two other female students assured me that we could continue to read and analyze "Retrospect for Life" as long as I didn't "make them talk," I felt the most uncomfortable and embarrassed that I ever had as a teacher. Part of my discomfort came from my overestimation of Hip-Hop Lit's ability to facilitate such personal conversations, as well as my unwitting invocation of male privilege More importantly, however, I worried that I had ruined my relationship with Keneka. After class, I read Keneka's journal entry for the day:

> I think if your not ready to have a baby or just don't want to have get a abortion but nine out of ten people would say its bad you do what you want to. So I would say abortion ok with me. Fuck it only you can make [several words scratched out] up your own mind.

Keneka's journal entry, which she represented in class simply by saying "yeah," provides further evidence that her resistance to the classroom activities of the day was not enacted to mask her lack of interest or effort. It seemed that Keneka had reflected a great deal about the topic and, as I would later find out, was putting forth great effort simply by remaining in the classroom.

I arrived at school early the following day hoping to catch Keneka in between classes so that we could talk about what had happened the previous day. I wanted to explain to her that much of what happened was a misunderstanding, and I wanted to apologize for any discomfort that I might have caused. I asked Ms. Blount, her first period teacher, if Keneka had come to her class and she told me that Keneka was absent. Although it was not uncommon for students to miss their first class and still come to Hip-Hop Lit, I was not optimistic. We were scheduled to discuss "Retrospect for Life" for another day and then move to "La Femme Fatal" by Digable Planets, in which the narrator politicizes and ultimately supports abortion, for 2 more days. Keneka, however, did not return to class for 7 days.

Due to unexpected scheduling issues, we were still reading "La Femme Fatal" when Keneka returned to school. Although Keneka did not express any dissonance with staying in the class, she was noticeably subdued. Even the normally vacant Mr. Colombo noted after the class that "Keneka was awful quiet today." I repeatedly looked at Keneka as

I taught the lesson to see if she was engaged in the activities. I found no answers in her face as she scribbled in her notebook and stared at her desk. Embarrassed and saddened by the experience, I canceled the remainder of the abortion section of the unit.

As several weeks passed, Keneka and I resumed our normal playful relationship. Nevertheless, I felt compelled to discuss the ordeal with her in order to express my apologies and understand her perspective. During one of our "make-up days," where students spent the entire period completing old assignments, I brought Keneka into the adjacent classroom and explained to her that it was not my intention to make her uncomfortable or force her to talk about overly personal information. She responded:

> I wasn't mad at you or nothin'. I just didn't want to talk. Remember in the summer time when you asked me if I was pregnant because I was getting fat? [I nodded] Well, I had got pregnant and I ain't wanna tell you. So when we was talking about it in class it just made me think. I had always said that it wouldn't happen to me and so I couldn't see myself like that.

Although our relationship was restored, this incident provided me with what I considered to be my greatest failure as an educator. Unbeknownst to me, I had created a painful situation for one of my students, completely undermining the goals of wounded healing. Further, the fact that another student, Haneef, had to intervene in order for me to recognize Keneka's silent suffering forced me to consider the other ways that Hip-Hop Lit potentially silenced all members of the community, even those who were typically willing to speak.

The story of Keneka represents the potential underside of Hip-Hop Lit and other sites of culturally relevant pedagogy. By linking the curriculum to the lived realities of students, particularly those from marginalized groups, we position ourselves to hear stories of pain, disappointment, and oppression that are often difficult to hear and even more difficult to tell. Given the commonality of many of these experiences among students and teachers, we must constantly consider how the articulation of their accompanying narratives can affect members of the storytelling community. Such a consideration demands that we listen not only to what is said in class, but also for silences and acts of silencing within the classroom.

TOWARD PEDAGOGIES OF HEALING

Even in the absence of an explicit focus on wounded healing, the effective use of culturally relevant curriculum and pedagogy inevitably creates new relationships between teachers, students, and the classroom context. Despite the well-documented virtues of such a shift, we must resist the urge to romanticize the relocation of previously marginalized cultural artifacts, epistemologies, and rituals into formal academic spaces. While such processes can yield extraordinary benefit, we must also take into account the problematic aspects of "culture" and the underside of "relevance." In particular, we must keep track of the ways in which many of our connections to culturally relevant texts are underwritten by stories of personal pain, forces of structural inequality, and sources of social misery. Although these realities should not necessarily disqualify such texts from entering the classroom, they demand that we move beyond merely hortatory approaches and adopt more critical postures.

Finally, the insights from this chapter force us to reimagine the classroom as a space in which teachers and students can "risk the self" through individual and collective storytelling. Although scholarship in fields such as composition theory and critical race theory advocate the use of storytelling, there remains a need to develop educational theory and practice that prepare us for the benefits, challenges, and consequences of enabling personal disclosures within the classroom. As this chapter demonstrates, the failure to take such considerations seriously severely undermines our ability to transform the classroom into a more safe, democratic, productive, and culturally responsive space.

5

||||||||||||||||||||||||||||||||||||||||||||||||||||||||||||||||||||||||||||||||||||||||||||||||

Bringing Back Sweet (and Not So Sweet) Memories

The Cultural Politics of Memory, Hip-Hop, and Generational Identity

"The history which bears and determines us has the form of a war rather than that of language: relations of power, not relations of meaning. History has no 'meaning,' though this is not to say that it is absurd or incoherent. On the contrary, it is intelligible and should be susceptible to analysis down to the smallest detail—but this in accordance with the intelligibility of struggles, of strategies and tactics."
—Michel Foucault, *Truth and Power*

"Like the faces that are woven in the fabric of my consciousness
To cities where makin' twenty one's a big accomplishment
To when my people understood their prominence
And my past life visions of the continent"
—Talib Kweli, "Memories Live"

Perhaps more than any other cultural movement, hip-hop is obsessed with its past. From the b-girl who rocks 1980s-style doorknocker earrings to the producer who "digs in the crates" to find the perfect old-school soul record, hip-hop culture is marked by a profound preoccupation with the recent and distant past. Such practices not only reflect but also shape the ways in which hip-hop culture positions us to "remember" the social world. While the act of remembering is often conceived as a personal one—a psychological process through which an individual retrieves information about the past—the study of collective memory points us to the "ideas, assumptions, and knowledges

99

that structure the relationship of individuals and groups to the immediate as well as the more distant past" (Sherman, 1999, p. 2).

This chapter examines the memory work that occurred within Hip-Hop Lit in response to the students' interactions with one of the course texts, "Things Done Changed" by rapper Notorious B.I.G. From this and other classroom texts, students were able to construct, contest, and reinscribe memories about the past. Through these memories, students reaffirmed and challenged particular social identities that informed and reflected their lived experiences. In particular, students in Hip-Hop Lit engaged in forms of collective remembering that reiterated and legitimated highly problematic public discourses surrounding the generational identity of today's youth. Although the initial classroom conversations were directly connected to our collective and individual readings of the Notorious B.I.G. text, this chapter looks more broadly at the students' construction and articulation of generational identities throughout the school year vis-à-vis their lived experiences.

COLLECTIVE MEMORY

Beginning with the pioneering work of Maurice Halbwachs (1992), and owing a conceptual debt to his mentor Emile Durkheim, scholars across the fields of sociology, anthropology, history, and cultural studies have examined how societies represent the past in ways that reflect the needs, concerns, and preoccupations of the present. In contrast to conventional approaches to history, which rely on empiricist notions of truth and objectivity about previous events (Wertsch, 2002), collective memory presumes the existence of multiple and frequently competing conceptions of the past. Further, the notion of collective memory politicizes the act of remembering by situating memories within the matrix of social practices.

In addition to its poststructuralist engagement with multiple narratives of the past, collective memory studies also focus on "memory texts" (Hodgkin & Radstone, 2003), or the variety of forms through which the past is represented within the public sphere. Through memory texts, which include television, film, museums, textbooks, and fashion (Samuel, 1994), memories accumulate and sustain political purchase in ways that benefit particular groups of people. For example, Olick (1999) demonstrates how German World War II commemoration ceremonies have influenced collective memory by shifting their emphasis from defeat to liberation, depending upon the political climate. Coontz (1992) and Lipsitz (1992) show how popular television and film construct collective memories and false nostalgia about the American past, particularly the 1950s. Such examples further evince the political nature of memory and remembering, as they are deployed to construct and contest various individual and social identities (Griffin, 2004).

The cultural politics of memory are particularly complicated within the current historical moment, which is marked by what Huyssen (1994, 2000) calls the "great paradox." Within high modernity, Huyssen argues, Western society is preoccupied with "time consciousness" (2000, p. 27), as evidenced by the increased focus on commemorations, memorializing, and historiography. At the same time, Western culture promotes forms of collective "forgetting" with regard to particular historical events, such as the Haitian revolution (Trouillot, 1995), American racism (Dyson, 2000), or the Jewish Holocaust (Silverman, 1999).

Collective memory is a central concept when examining the cultural politics of HHBE. As critical educational theorists have argued (e.g., Apple, 1993; Bowles & Gintis, 1976), one of the primary functions of modern schools is to sanction particular forms of knowledge that privilege the interests of dominant groups. Through this process, particular memories of the past become central to our conceptions of ourselves and the world in which we are situated, while other memories are inevitably marginalized or completely submerged, thereby facilitating the construction of social identities that hinge upon unawareness of, indifference to, or complicity with various forms of oppression. With regard to schooling, the study of collective memory demands an analysis of the ways in which the official narratives of school delimit and produce possibilities for understanding the past in ways that allow for the constitution of various identities. An equally critical approach to HHBE demands an analysis of the pedagogical role that hip-hop texts and cultural workers play in the lives of youth by offering particular narratives of the past as "public pedagogy" (Trofanenko, 2006).

Despite the problematic possibilities and uses of collective memory, it is important not to view it through a deficit lens. As Bissell (2005) argues, such approaches to collective memory, and nostalgia in particular, have undermined scholarly treatment of the subject:

From the social sciences to cultural studies and the humanities, nostalgia has generally been understood as perverse, if not pathological. It has been closely associated with a specifically counter-Enlightenment tradition, embraced by nationalists and romantics alike. Tinged with echoes of Herder and Rousseau, it is typically dismissed as antimodern and regressive. As a legacy of the gendered terms of classical social thought, nostalgia has also been viewed as an emotional affair and hence regarded as irrational. . . . As a false or fictitious history, the product of fantasy, nostalgia lacks a "proper" distance or objectivity. Moreover, it is typically represented as a reaction to a larger and more encompassing set of forces: modernity or modernization; consumption, spectacle, and the eclipse of history; postmodernism; transnational or late capitalism; and, of course, globalization. (pp. 224–225)

For anthropologists, viewing particular forms of memory work such as nostalgia, as "errors" committed by "native" populations who lack the critical faculties to make sense of their condition, has problematic methodological and theoretical consequences. From such a paternalistic and colonizing posture, we are unequipped to locate the sophisticated range of ways by which people use forms of remembering in response to historically specific circumstances. This is not to ignore or understate the relationship between memory work and the maintenance of relations of power that operate against the interests of particular groups. Rather, it is equally important that ethnographic analyses locate sites of critical reflection and resistance within particular communities, accounting for the ways that people use particular memories in order to endure, challenge, or transform their circumstances. It is from this perspective that I examine the ways in which students in Hip-Hop Lit engaged narratives of the past in order to construct complex and often contradictory generational identities.

NEGOTIATING GENERATIONAL IDENTITY

As a part of our unit on The Hood, in which the class read various texts that examined urban neighborhoods from a variety of perspectives (celebratory, critical, etc.), I selected "Things Done Changed" by Notorious B.I.G., a.k.a. Biggie Smalls (1994). While many of the course texts were written by less popular artists, I chose "Things Done Changed" despite Notorious B.I.G.'s status (both before and after his violent death) as one of hip-hop's most critically and commercially celebrated artists. My primary reasons for choosing the piece were its rich description of the urban ghetto and its relatively obscure status within Notorious B.I.G.'s oeuvre; most of the students had not encountered "Things Done Changed" despite being self-professed "Biggie fans." These two factors were critical, as I anticipated that students would benefit from the text both as literature and as a way to deepen their understanding of one of their favorite artists. Despite his generally acclaimed talent, Notorious B.I.G.'s work is typically associated with wanton consumerism, violence, and sexism, thereby obscuring what I believed to be its more introspective and political dimensions. For this reason, I asked the class to read "Things Done Changed" in its entirety in an effort to demonstrate the complexity of Notorious B.I.G. and his work:

> Remember back in the days, when niggaz had waves
> Gazelle shades, and corn braids
> Pitchin pennies, honies had the high top jellies
> Shootin skelly, motherfuckers was all friendly
> Loungin at the barbeques, drinkin brews
> With the neighborhood crews, hangin on the avenues
> Turn your pagers, to nineteen ninety three
> Niggaz is getting' smoked G, believe me
> Talk slick, you get your neck slit quick
> Cause real street niggaz ain't havin' that shit
> Totin techs for rep, smokin' blunts in the project
> hallways, shootin dice all day
> Wait for niggaz to step up on some fightin' shit
> We get hype and shit and start lightin' shit
> So step away with your fistfight ways
> Motherfucker this ain't back in the days, but you don't hear me
>   though
>
> No more cocoa leave-io, one two three
> One two three, all of this to me, is a mystery
> I hear you motherfuckers talk about it
> But I stay seein' bodies with the motherfuckin' chalk around it
> And I'm down with the shit too
> For the stupid motherfuckers wanna try to use Kung-Fu

Instead of a Mac-10 he tried scrappin'
Slugs in his back and, that's what the fuck happens
When you sleep on the street
Little motherfuckers with heat, want to leave a nigga six feet
    deep
And we comin' to the wake
To make sure the cryin' and commotion ain't a motherfuckin'
    fake
Back in the days, our parents used to take care of us
Look at 'em now, they even fuckin' scared of us
Callin' the city for help because they can't maintain
Damn, shit done changed

If I wasn't in the rap game
I'd probably have a key knee deep in the crack game
Because the streets is a short stop
Either you're slingin' crack rock or you got a wicked jumpshot
Shit, it's hard being young from the slums
Eatin five cent gums not knowin' where your meals comin'
    from
And now the shit's gettin' crazier and major
Kids younger than me, they got the Sky Grand Pagers
Goin' outta town, blowin' up
Six months later all the dead bodies showin' up
It make me wanna grab the nine and the shottie
But I gotta go identify the body
Damn, what happened to the summertime cookouts?
Everytime I turn around a nigga gettin' took out
Shit, my momma got cancer in her breast
Don't ask me why I'm motherfuckin' stressed, things done
    changed

After reading "Things Done Changed" as a group, we began a class-room discussion. I was primarily interested in highlighting Notorious B.I.G.'s analysis of the social forces that created the conditions that he describes in the song. I posed a question to the class about the theme of the piece: "What was Biggie trying to say in the song?" Without hesita-tion, Dorene, one of the students in Hip-Hop Lit, responded, "We ain't shit!" Both amused and intrigued by her response, I engaged her and a few others in dialogue:

Me: How did he say that "we ain't shit"?
Dorene: Not us [gesturing with her pointer fingers to represent the entire class]. *Us!* Not you and Colombo. Kids nowadays is different.

I resisted the urge to point out to Dorene that I was less than 10 years older than all of the students and that "Things Done Changed" was released in 1994, nearly 10 years before these students would read it. As such, the song was more reflective of my peers than theirs. Instead, I tried to push them further:

Me: How are they different?
Dorene: Like Biggie said, we crazy! [pauses as class laughs] I'm serious!
Jay: Exactly. Like when he say, "Wait for niggaz to step up on some fightin' shit / We get hype and shit / And start lightin' shit." We don't rumble no more. We shoot!
Me: What else?
Keneka: Our generation just don't care!
Me: How so?
Keneka: Most of us don't care. We having kids and we kids our damn self. We smoke weed all the time, hanging out on the corner, just not caring.

By the end of the class, the students had provided me with an exhaustive list of their generation's shortcomings. Surprised, I wrote the following in my field notes after the class had ended:

After reading the Biggie piece, the students seemed to interpret it as proof that their generation (really my generation) is somehow worse than others. When I asked for evidence, the students reminded me of [conservative pundits] Bill O'Reilly or Rush Limbaugh as they talked about drugs, violence, and babies. I'm curious to know what causes them to feel that way.

Throughout the semester, the students continued (as they had before this lesson) to articulate various dimensions of a *generational identity*, or the beliefs, values, experiences, and narratives that bind a particular age cohort. As scholars have noted, generational identity is a by-product of generational memory, which "grows out of social interactions that are in the first place historical and collective and later internalized in a deeply visceral and unconscious way so as to dictate vital choices and control reflexes of loyalty" (Nora, 1996, p. 526). For many of the students in the class, their conceptions of generational identity mirrored the sentiments of those who view youth as victims of what West (1993) calls "walking nihilism," or a profound sense of meaninglessness that undermines personal fulfillment and productive engagement with democratic life.

While this notion of walking nihilism was an immediately apparent textual theme, I did not anticipate that the students would interpret "Things Done Changed" in ways that corroborated the nostalgic narratives of the past that they would appeal to throughout the school year in articulating their own generational identities. Closer examination, however, reveals how "Things Done Changed," like many other hip-hop texts within and outside of Hip-Hop Lit, served as a memory text that reflected and reinforced the students' complex sense of generational identity.

HISTORICAL EXCEPTIONALISM

In "Things Done Changed," Notorious B.I.G. draws a sharp distinction between adolescents in the 1980s and those in 1993, the year to which he devotes his primary narrative attention within the text. Like many of the texts that we read in class, such as "Year of the Dragon" by Wyclef Jean and Lauryn Hill and "Doo Rags" by Nas, "Things Done Changed" constructs contemporary youth as drastically different from their predecessors. Further, Notorious B.I.G. ascribes a sense of "historical exceptionalism," or the belief that an event is "so unique and unprecedented as to transcend time and defy comparison or historical analysis" (Kaplan, 2003, p. 56), onto himself and his peers. Through claims of historical exceptionalism, "Things Done Changed" and other such texts tacitly assert that current youth face heretofore unseen social conditions and pressures that demand new subjectivities, worldviews, and social practices. Throughout the semester, the students consistently conveyed a similar sense of generational identity that reflected a feeling of historical exceptionalism in relationship to other generational cohorts.

While the students never explicitly referred to the popular labels given to other generations by the academy and popular media, such as "baby boomer" for those born between 1946 and 1964 (Weiss, 2000) or "hip-hop generation" for those born between 1965 and 1984 (Kitwana, 2002), they expressed a keen (though inexact) historical sensibility with regard to the existential distance between their generation and recent predecessors. This was often demonstrated through the clear distinctions that students made between other relatively young people (such as myself) and themselves. As Josh noted, "We're different than our old-heads. Even the ones who just went through it." Lisa explained further:

> Like, my mom had me when she was real young, like fourteen, so it's not like we that different. But at the same time, y'ah mean, we totally different. We don't look at stuff the same way. That's because we from a different generation.

When pressed about the factors that created such sharp differences between their immediate predecessors and themselves, the students made arguments for historical exceptionalism similar to those expressed in "Things Done Changed." A few weeks after completing the unit, I had a conversation with a few of the students in the class that reflected this sentiment:

> *Me*: When we were reading Biggie, most of y'all agreed with him that your generation is different. Why do y'all think that you're so different?
> *Jay*: We have to go through different shit.
> *Me*: Like what kinda stuff?
> *Jay*: Drugs, killings, babies. All that shit.
> *Me*: And you don't think that other generations had to go through this?
> *Jay*: Not the same way.
> *Dorene*: Like, back in the day they was smoking weed. But we got smokers [crack addicts]. People was having babies but not all like that. It's out of control now.
> *Shaheem*: Word. We act different 'cause we gotta deal wit' different shit. Y'all ain't have to worry about drug dealers and drive-by's and shit.

In a different conversation, Kwame added:

> A lot of times my oldheads like my brother and niggas around the way be coming at me trying to school me to shit

and sometimes they just be talking about how young boahs
is crazy. I respect them and everything but they don't understand . . . that shit ain't like before. We act how we act 'cause
shit ain't like before.

These comments were reflective of the dominant belief within Hip-
Hop Lit that the students faced a unique set of social circumstances.
Further, the chronological bounds of their generational cohort excluded "oldheads" like me, who in reality were not much older than
them.

In many ways, the students' sense of historical exceptionalism demonstrates their keen understanding of the relationship between social
conditions and individual behavior. Rather than merely linking their
generation's ostensibly bad behavior to biological defect or arbitrary
decision-making, they frequently conveyed a belief that their daily
experiences and identities were shaped by troubling aspects of the
current social landscape such as drug dealers and drive-by shootings.
On the other hand, the belief that such conditions were historically
unprecedented supported the students' articulated feelings of moral
inferiority, or the belief that previous generations held a moral authority over them based on the quality of their lived responses to the social
conditions that they faced.

MORAL INFERIORITY

In "Things Done Changed," Notorious B.I.G. paints an image of morally estranged, nihilistic youth engaged in self-destructive acts such
as substance abuse and wanton violence. Further, he articulates a feeling of severe social disjuncture between his peers and adults—parents
who raise their children but now see them as threats in their adolescence. In this regard, Notorious B.I.G. echoes many of the dominant
discourses surrounding youth that have constructed them as out-of-
control and hopeless civic terrors (Dimitriadis, 2001; Giroux, 1996,
2004).

Much of the discourse within Hip-Hop Lit reflected a similar belief
that the students' generation was morally inferior to its predecessors.
This is evidenced by their frequent claims that they were engaged in
levels of violence, sexual promiscuity, and substance abuse that were
considerably greater than those of their predecessors. Paradoxically,

while the students acknowledged their unique historical position, their comments reflected the belief that they, and not their allegedly unique historical circumstances, were largely to blame for their ostensible moral shortcomings. An excellent example of this contradiction came a few weeks after we read "Things Done Changed" and Josh matter-of-factly alluded to his generation's moral inferiority:

Josh: You know how this generation is worse than the last. Well, that's . . .

Me: Wait. What do you mean worse?

Josh: We do more shit. Like, we do all kinds of messed-up stuff . . .

Me: You don't think that your parents did messed-up stuff?

Josh: Yeah, but it's different. For one, we do it more worse. Plus we don't do shit 'cause we don't know no better. We just don't give a "f."

Me: Give me an example.

Josh: [pauses thoughtfully] Okay. Like back in the day y'all used to smoke crack. . . . [laughter] Not you, but you know what I mean. Y'all ain't know that it was that bad 'cause it just came out. But now, we see how f'ed up people get from smoking. . . . Losin' they teeth, trickin' and everything. And it's niggas that still do it!

Me: Hold on, so you think that people who smoke crack do it because they know it's bad and just don't care?

Dorene: Yeah! Just like they know they gonna get pregnant if they have sex without no condom. But they still do it. [louder] We don't give a fuck!

The above vignette speaks to the students' tendency to both internalize and literally echo the dominant discourses about current youth that, as Giroux (1997) points out, "shifts from an emphasis on social failings in the society to questions of individual character . . . from the language of social investment . . . to the language of containment and blame" (p. 17). The students in Hip-Hop Lit rarely explicitly acknowledged the relationship between their self-described moral inferiority and any structural conditions that may have helped to create it. When I challenged them by raising such issues myself, they typically dismissed my comments as excuses or exaggerations. For example, in the above exchange, I responded to Dorene by saying:

Me: There are a whole lotta people who don't know how to
practice safe sex. Plus, even if you know about it, it might be
reasons why you don't do it.
Dorene: That's what I'm sayin'! They don't care!
Me: Naw. You're missing me. I'm saying it's not that simple.
What if you grew up without anybody in the house that
loved you? A lot of people say that they have babies because
they wanted somebody to love them.
Dorene: That's B.S. I had a baby because I ain't like the way the
condoms was feelin'. [class laughs]
Jay: Exactly. Back in the day that ain't happen all like that. And
if it did, you got married.

Dorene's unwillingness to acknowledge the legitimacy of factors
other than individual irresponsibility in teenage pregnancy reflected the students' belief that, while real, structural impediments (e.g.,
abstinence-only sex education courses, sex-driven media texts) were
drastically less significant than individual choice and responsibility.
To many of them, their failures were due to an inability to appropriately respond to their unique social circumstances. Equally important,
however, was Jay's response, which reflected the students' tendency
to appeal to the past to legitimate their conceptions of generational
identity.

"REMEMBERING" THE RECENT PAST

The conception of generational identity that pervades "Things Done
Changed" is informed by nostalgic narratives of the "recent past," or
the last 50 years. In the song, Notorious B.I.G. invokes nostalgic memories of the early 1980s, such as summertime cookouts, neighborhood
unity, and strong parent–child relationships, all of which are held in
narrative contradistinction to his analysis of his own generation. At
the same time, he submerges other memories of the decade such as the
resurgence of gang violence, rising suicide rates, the evaporation of the
welfare state, and the development of crack economies within postindustrial urban spaces. Through this practice, Notorious B.I.G. is able
to elaborately construct an apocalyptic narrative about his peers and
himself. As a result, "Things Done Changed" reflects the nostalgic im-
pulse that pervades many cultural texts, as well as the broader public

and counterpublic discourses that informed the Hip-Hop Lit students' conceptions of generational identity.

The conceptions of generational identity articulated by students in Hip-Hop Lit were similarly shaped by their collective memories of the recent past. Throughout the year, students would often appeal to nostalgic narratives of the past 50 years in order to substantiate claims about their own generation. Through these acts of remembering, they were able to defend themselves from my scrutiny. A typical instance of this came during our Family unit, where we read "Where Have You Been" by Beanie Sigel and Jay-Z. Our reading of the text, in which the rappers write angry letters to their absentee fathers, triggered a conversation about the condition of the modern family:

Dorene: That's why kids is messed up now.
Me: What you mean?
Dorene: Families don't stick together no more.
Me: Why do you think that is?
Joe: Back in the day, you had everybody in one house. Now it's like everybody get divorced or they don't even get married in the first place.

Later in the class, Shaheem commented:

Kids now days is accidents. You know how back in the day you get married, you have kids and shit? Now y'all just get it in and if she get pregnant you deal with it. . . . You take care of your seed or you don't but either way you doin' it before y'all married. That's the problem.

As the above passages demonstrate, the students' conceptions of generational identity were, at least in part, constructed in relationship to their memories of the recent past. In the above case, the recent past represented a historical moment of familial strength and unity, as well as sexual morality. Consequently, the students accepted highly questionable memories of a pristine American family that, as Coontz (1992) points out, never truly existed: "Like most visions of a 'golden age,' the 'traditional family' evaporates on closer examination. It is an ahistorical amalgam of structures, values, and behaviors that never coexisted in the same time and place" (p. 9). For example, the popular belief that today's youth engage in more premarital sex than earlier generations is effectively countered by higher infant mortality rates, younger marriages, and more liberal sexual consent laws within today's society (Coontz, 1992; Cutwright, 1972). Nevertheless, such historical distortions legitimate nostalgic memories of the recent past that allow youth to construct the present and the future through a discourse of decline.

Although the students were mostly critical of their own generation, they also unfavorably evaluated their immediate predecessors (parents, "oldheads", etc.) in relation to their memories of the "civil rights generation." As Kwame joked, "Back in the day they had Martin Luther King and Malcolm X. We got Biggie and 'Pac." He later elaborated:

> It's not like before. You know how back in the day everybody was fightin' for the same thing? Now everybody doin' they own thing. They don't care about racism and drugs and all that. Everybody tryin' to get theirs. That's why don't nothin' get done.

Kwame's comments echoed the class's primary sentiment that history moves along a sliding scale where heroism, morality, and social activism dissipate with every emerging generation.

It is worth reiterating that the students' nostalgic appeals to the past for cultural ideals are neither uncommon nor thoroughly dysfunctional practices. As many scholars have noted (e.g., Coontz, 1992; Hirsch & Spitzer, 2003), the idealization of past time and lost place is a common cultural practice within late modernity. While some have critiqued nostalgia as a "retrospective mirage that greatly simplifies, if not falsifies, the past" (Spitzer, 1998, p. 20), others have spotlighted the functionality of such a practice for developing "a resistant relationship to the present . . . that envisions a better future" (Bal, 1999, p. 72). Through nostalgia, communities are able to engage in individual and collective self-critique, sustain moral traditions, and imagine a better future.

In the case of Hip-Hop Lit, the students' nostalgic memory work represented more than low generational self-esteem, but also a means by which to engage in self-critique and prompt activism with regard to the very issues that they were raising as problematic. For example, Kwame and Shaheem, two of the most vocal students regarding generational inferiority, were also engaged in community activism related to AIDS awareness and abstinence-only education, respectively. Also,

Jay served as a basketball coach and mentor to younger students at the local community center. In a journal entry during the Family unit, Jay wrote:

> A lot people my age don't have mentors or fathers or anything because everybody's locked up or just doesn't care. That's why I decided to be a basketball coach. I can help a young man be something better by telling him not to get caught up in foolishness.

As such, many of the students' pessimistic critiques about the state of leadership and moral efficacy within their generation were betrayed by their own actions. Although their activism would have nonetheless benefited from a more historically complex and redemptive analysis of their generation—perhaps, for example, prompting them to recognize and contribute to structural as well as individual changes within the context of their community involvement—such practices force us to look beyond a merely deficit analysis of the students' memory work. Rather than viewing their memory work as an example of false consciousness, we must consider the various ways that particular narratives of the past, however "untrue," offer pragmatic and redemptive possibilities for youth.

LOCATING MEMORIES

As I have argued throughout this chapter, there were numerous points of contact between the students' conceptions of generational identity and the themes that emerge from a close reading of "Things Done Changed." It is important to reiterate, however, that these connections were not limited to the Notorious B.I.G. text, nor were they apparent only at the level of formal data analysis. Rather, the students often acknowledged the influence of a wide range of media texts on their conceptions of generational identity at the same time that they articulated them.

Although "Things Done Changed" became central to our conversations, as the students and I frequently referenced it throughout the year, other texts were also used to validate the students' constructions of generational identity vis-à-vis collective remembering. Students would often refer to popular media texts in order to validate their claims about the recent past. For example, several students referred to the popular 1980s television series *The Cosby Show* and the 1970s series *Good Times* as evidence of the familial stability of previous generations. Such references were often uncritical, as the students rarely questioned the legitimacy or accuracy of the texts in their constructions of the past. This was the case in the following comment from Robin about the condition of families:

> You know how back in the day, like on *The Cosby Show*, how the mom would be there and Bill Cosby would be there and everybody and the kids was all good? I mean . . . they wasn't perfect but now you got shows like *The Parkers* where it's just Monique and her daughter. That's what I'm talkin' 'bout.

While insightful, Robin's comparison of *The Cosby Show* and *The Parkers*, a sitcom about a working-class African American single mother and her daughter, reflects the students' tendency to accept and make use of the texts that validated their claims without engaging in critical analyses from which viable alternatives could emerge. In this case, Robin made use of *The Cosby Show* to provide evidence of a stable family in the recent past while ignoring the existence of other shows like *What's Happening* or *Diff'rent Strokes*, which offered alternate conceptions of the family unit—a single African American mother raising two children in the first example and a single White man raising two adopted African American children and his own White child in the second example—within the same historical moment. In doing this, Robin tacitly acknowledged the contribution of media texts in constructing her understanding of the past without calling into question the arbitrary choice of the texts that she depended on for her particular memories.

In addition to referencing media texts as legitimate sources of memory, the students also directly appropriated the language and sentiment of many popular texts in articulating their opinions. For example, Kwame's joke about Notorious B.I.G. and Tupac being the leaders of his generation as opposed to Martin Luther King and Malcolm X was taken from a routine made famous by comedian Chris Rock. Again, such comments reflect the students' dependence on the memories contained within media texts in constructing both the past and their conceptions of generational identity, as well as their frequent unwillingness to critically interrogate the sources of their memories.

Although the students' memories of the recent past were shaped by "Things Done Changed" and other media texts, they were also constructed through their interactions with their elders. One day, during a class discussion in which I was particularly frustrated by the students' comments, I gained tremendous insight into the sources of their memories:

Me: Where do y'all get this stuff from? . . . I mean, y'all always talking about how it used to be, like y'all sixty years old or somethin'. Is anything better now?

Josh: I mean, I ain't sayin' it's all bad now but it was better before. Like, when you talk to oldheads, they always talk about how stuff is worse now.

Shaheem: You know how you be talking to your grandmom and she be like [mimics an elderly African American woman] "When I was a kid, we wasn't allowed to do shit. *That's* y'all problem, you got it too easy"? [laughter] For real, though. You don't be wantin' to hear that shit sometime but you know she right.

Me: Do y'all get that a lot from older people?

Shaheem: Yeah. They always be like "Things were better back then."

Lisa: My grandmom be sayin' the same stuff.

Me: Damn, now that you mention it. Mine did too!

The above conversation not only further demonstrates the social nature of students' memories about the recent past, but also their own recognition that many of their memories were constructed through social interactions.

HIP-HOP LIT AS MEMORY TEXT

Despite their sophisticated understanding of the socially constructed nature of memory, as well their complex engagement with particular narratives, the students in Hip-Hop Lit were still extremely reluctant to fully relinquish their preexisting conceptions of the past and themselves. It is important, however, not to reduce the students' perspectives to stubbornness or false consciousness. In addition to obscuring the complexity and functionality of their memory work, such a reading would ignore the ways in which the curriculum and pedagogy of the Hip-Hop Lit context helped to constitute the classroom itself as a contradictory memory text that reinforced the very ideas that I attempted to challenge.

One of the primary ways that Hip-Hop Lit operated as a memory text was through the curriculum. Every course text that discussed the past or assessed current youth did so from a nostalgic position: "Summertime" by the Fresh Prince was an extremely nostalgic ode to "old school" summers; "Year of the Dragon" by Wyclef and Lauryn Hill appealed to idyllic childhood memories in its critique of modern societal conditions; and Common's "I Used to Love H.E.R." deployed the sexist metaphor of a young girl to detail hip-hop culture's shift from "pure and untampered" to "the sewer." Based on their lyrical content, the course texts did very little to challenge the students' memories of the recent past or their conceptions of generational identity. Rather than using texts by hip-hop artists such as Ras Kass, The Coup, or KRS-One, all of whose work provides critical challenges to nostalgic narratives of the past, my selection of course texts reinforced the very things that I found problematic. As such, my pedagogical attempts at challenging students' expressed conceptions of generational identity were constantly undermined by the curriculum that I co-constructed.

As several students expressed toward the end of the school year, it was the frequent contradiction between the course texts and my classroom pedagogy that undermined my attempts at challenging their conceptions of generational identity. Josh reinforced this point during a postsemester interview:

> *Josh*: A lot of times it seemed like you were just pushing us to think deep about stuff. You ain't really mean what you was sayin'.
> *Me*: Why you say that?
> *Josh*: The whole class be saying one thing. Even Mr. Colombo don't really be disagreeing with us. But you be steady acting like we wrong.
> *Me*: [laughing] Maybe *all* y'all wrong!!
> *Josh*: [laughing] How we all wrong? The rappers wrong too?
> *Me*: Naw, it's not even really about "wrong." It's . . .
> *Josh*: I understand. You wanted to challenge us so we wouldn't

believe everything we read, even from hip-hop. *We are still in school!* [emphasis added]

As Josh's comments suggest, one of the primary purposes of Hip-Hop Lit was to demonstrate the legitimacy of hip-hop texts and artists as sources of "official knowledge." Given this explicit goal, as well the content of the course texts, Josh and many of his colleagues interpreted my challenges as teaching strategies designed to reinforce the truth-value of the texts.

Josh's final comment ("We *are* still in school!") speaks to the particular ways in which, despite my attempts to construct the classroom as a counter-hegemonic space, the students viewed the relationship between Hip-Hop Lit and the broader schooling context. Although the students viewed Hip-Hop Lit as a unique and unconventional learning space, many students still saw it as a place for advancing the traditional imperatives of schooling. For example, during a class discussion, several students echoed Lisa's comment that "[T]his class is good because we learn a lot about ourselves and we learn what we're supposed to learn in a way we can relate to." Although the notion of celebrating hip-hop culture and scaffolding traditional disciplinary knowledge were explicit aims of the course, I also viewed the course as a site for challenging the political and epistemological underpinnings of formal schooling. As Maggie's post-semester remarks suggest, however, this latter point was not fully conveyed through my course:

> I know that this class was supposed to make us better so that we can finish school and do good in our lives. I think that's why they hired you . . . 'cause they knew you could relate to us and get us to do the right things.

Although I saw Hip-Hop Lit as a place for reimagining the possibilities of formal schooling, Maggie's comments reflect a dominant sense that the Hip-Hop Lit course was developed to help students adjust to the everyday logic of school. This belief was likely intensified by the fact that the Twilight Program is often considered a "last-chance" program for "at-risk" youth. As a result, many students saw my challenges—which were contradicted by the course texts, curriculum, and broader media landscape—as an attempt to make them feel better about themselves rather than countervailing the dominant antiyouth discourse.

REMEMBERING FORWARD

While some of the contradictions that emerged in Hip-Hop Lit could have been addressed at the level of curriculum design—e.g., carefully choosing texts based on their content—it is equally important to consider how youth inevitably approach hip-hop and other popular culture texts in ways that defy the expectations of critics, scholars, teachers, and other adults. As discussed throughout this chapter, the particular ways in which youth use popular texts to craft identities and inform worldviews emerge from concrete relations of power. In order to account for these specific circumstances, HHBE scholars and practitioners must resist the urge to develop, implement, and critique educational projects in the absence of youth. Instead, we must work *with* youth to construct educational contexts that respond to their particular circumstances as well as broader global forces.

Finally, the type of identity work performed by the students in response to "Things Done Changed" speaks to the pedagogical role of hip-hop and other media texts in constructing the particular versions of the past that students appeal to when making sense of their current conditions, as well as their possibilities for the future. For educators, whether or not they are engaged in HHBE, the insights of this case suggest that educators should engage in a close and deliberate analysis of the various memories inscribed in both popular and traditional classroom texts: How is the past constructed within the text? How is this particular version of the past connected to or disconnected from the lived experiences of the students? What are the consequences of confirming or challenging such memories? Such an analysis is critical for connecting to the experiences of students, as well as to the explicit and tacit ideologies that inform classroom pedagogy.

6

||||||||||||||||||||||||||||||||||||||||||||||||||||||||||||||||||||||||||||||||||||||||||||||||||||

Stakes Is High
(The Remix)

Toward a Hip-Hop Pedagogy

"Although the progressive educational movements of the 1960s
and 1970s helped to inaugurate a number of important legislative
programs, they often exaggerated the concept of personal freedom,
which at times collapsed into a form of vapid anti-intellectualism;
they often legitimated infantile as opposed to mature forms of
scholarship; moreover they argued for a child-centered pedagogy
which amounted to a romantic celebration of student culture and
experience that made progressive reform patterns seem unrealistic."
—Henry Giroux and Peter McLaren,
"Schooling, Cultural Politics and the Struggle for Democracy"

"Stakes is high like my uncle is
We both got problems, he never confronted his"
—Common, "Time Traveling"

At the end of the school year, as I was finishing my exit interviews with
the students, I bumped into Mr. Ormond in the hallway. "I'm glad I
caught you before you left," he said, giving me a hearty handshake
and hug. After thanking me for my work, his tone quickly shifted from
lighthearted to serious. "What do we do now?" he asked with a look
of genuine concern. Before I could respond, he continued, "Everything
that happened here was so great. But how can we do it again?" The
urgency of Mr. Ormond's questions, which are a constant reminder of
the stakes attached to hip-hop–based education, continue to prod me
as I write this final chapter.

At the beginning of this book, I raised several critical questions
about hip-hop–based education (HHBE): "Why does it work?," "For

whom does it work?," and "What's at stake when it works?" Throughout this book, I have taken up these questions by demonstrating how knowledge, power, and identities are (re)negotiated within HHBE contexts. With each chapter, I have attempted to provide new layers of access to the rich, varied, and often unpredictable relationships that young people forge with hip-hop texts within the classroom context. In this final chapter, I leverage these insights in order to develop and articulate a *hip-hop pedagogy* that not only amplifies my response to the aforementioned questions, but also speaks to the "What do we do now?" question that is often raised by educational theorists, researchers, and, most importantly, practitioners like Mr. Ormond.

By hip-hop pedagogy, I am not suggesting a prefigured set of strategies or activities for reaching students through hip-hop culture. As I have demonstrated throughout this book, such strategies are inevitably defied by the everyday identity work of students and teachers. Rather, hip-hop pedagogy reflects an alternate, more expansive vision of pedagogy that reconsiders the relationships among students, teachers, texts, schools, and the broader social world. To illuminate this vision, I focus on three distinct but interrelated forms of hip-hop pedagogy: pedagogies *of* hip-hop; pedagogies *about* hip-hop; and pedagogies *with* hip-hop.

PEDAGOGIES *OF* HIP-HOP

Drawing from McLaren's (1989) definition of pedagogy as the "introduction to, preparation for, and legitimation of particular forms of social life" (p. 160), pedagogies of hip-hop reflect the various ways that hip-hop culture authorizes particular values, truth claims, and subject positions while implicitly or explicitly contesting others. By framing these issues as fundamentally pedagogical, we become theoretically equipped to frame practitioners of hip-hop as engaged cultural workers, critical intellectuals, and public pedagogues whose intellectual production both reflects and constitutes a variety of identities, discourses, and power relationships.

While this book has focused primarily on printed rap texts, pedagogies of hip-hop extend beyond traditional notions of text and reach into all aspects of hip-hop cultural production. From the hypermasculine performances of Tupac to the postmodern racial authenticity politics of Eminem to the transnational economy of hip-hop aesthetics, the pedagogy of hip-hop highlights the ways in which hip-hop culture plays a "formative role in shaping the social identities of youth" (Giroux, 1994, p. 178). Furthermore, it points to the broader sectors of popular culture, such as street fiction novels (Hill, Perez, & Irby, 2008), urban fashion (Fleetwood, 2005), and double dutch games (Gaunt, 2006), that are shaped by the cultural logic and stylistic etiquette of hip-hop culture.

Throughout this book, I have highlighted how youth often consume and produce hip-hop culture in ways that reorganize their conceptions of themselves and the world around them. Often, these practices not only defy *a priori* analyses, but also radically challenge sanctioned formations of knowledge and produce new categories of meaning. By examining these practices as part of a pedagogical process, we are better positioned to locate the unique knowledge claims, aesthetic practices, and habits of mind and body that are indigenous to hip-hop culture. These practices, which Petchauer (in press) refers to as a "hip-hop world view," demonstrate how hip-hop culture is not merely a derivative or reactionary cultural form, but a rich and dynamic site of authentic cultural production.

In order to fully understand the pedagogical power of hip-hop, our intellectual energy cannot merely be exhausted at the level of textual analysis. Instead, scholars, critics, and everyday observers must also consider the relationships between hip-hop culture and the ever-expanding range of economic, political, and social arrangements that shape its consumption and production. Furthermore, as I argued in the opening chapter, these conditions must be studied within the context of everyday engagements with hip-hop culture. This type of analysis requires not only rigorous textual exegeses, but also rich and varied ethnographic accounts of the dynamic and often unpredictable relationships that individuals forge with hip-hop culture.

Although an understanding of the pedagogy of hip-hop presumes that hip-hop culture is a fecund intellectual space, we must resist the urge to romanticize its insights. As this book has demonstrated, hip-hop culture is not, nor could ever be, a space for purely transgressive, revolutionary, or even resistant practice. Rather, it operates as a terrain of struggle over competing meanings, values, and truth claims. A deep understanding of this terrain is critical for unpacking the pedagogies of hip-hop, as well as positioning us for engaging in pedagogies *about* hip-hop.

PEDAGOGIES *ABOUT* HIP-HOP

Although it was not the primary educational objective of the course, the Hip-Hop Lit classroom offered a space where students could engage in critical conversations about the cultural texts that they consumed within and outside the classroom. These conversations partially constitute what I refer to as "pedagogies *about* hip-hop," or the use of educational spaces to analyze, critique, and (re)produce hip-hop texts. When engaging in pedagogies about hip-hop, students and teachers operate as cultural critics who deploy critical literacies in order to identify and respond to structures of power and meaning within hip-hop texts.

As I have demonstrated throughout this book, pedagogies about hip-hop are necessary features not only of preplanned curricular events, but also ordinary educational practice. While discrete units on critical media literacy are significant, it is within the "rhythm of the ordinary" that students and teachers often offer their most sincere and profound perspectives. Furthermore, given the salience of hip-hop culture within the lives of many students, pedagogies about hip-hop cannot be restricted to hip-hop–based curricula, but also must be included in more traditional educational programming. In such contexts, which comprise the overwhelming majority of students' schooling lives, teachers must be willing and prepared to mine traditional curriculum and pedagogy for "sites of possibility" (Hill & Vasudevan, 2008) for pedagogies about hip-hop. To do this, teachers must not only pay careful attention to the words and actions of students, but also to the broader universe of meaning described in the aforementioned section.

As the case of Hip-Hop Lit has taught us, an engagement with pedagogies about hip-hop produces considerable tensions, dilemmas, and contradictions within the classroom. By challenging the students' beliefs about topics such as race, class, gender, and sexuality through their analyses of hip-hop texts, they are often forced to explain their allegiances to particular texts, perspectives, and interests. Also, given the resonance of particular texts and conversations with their lived experiences, students will often be forced to confess their beliefs, desires, fears, and traumas in full public view. Such moments will often place students into a defensive posture that compromises the safe and democratic spaces that hip-hop pedagogies aim to construct.

For this reason, teachers must resist the urge to position themselves as sole arbiters of culture when engaging in critical dialogues with students. This is not to suggest that the troubling aspects of hip-hop culture, such as misogyny, homophobia, and consumerism, should not be called into question. Indeed, such critique is an unavoidable aspect of any morally and ethically credible pedagogical project. Rather, the critical dialogues that take place between teachers and students surrounding hip-hop culture must not degenerate into a school-sanctioned attack on students' lives and values. To avoid this tendency, teachers must assume a posture of what Schultz (2003) has called "deep listening," which moves them away from "listening *in* on students" and toward listening "*for* understanding" (p. 105). Nevertheless, even under the most optimal conditions, the practice of pedagogies about hip-hop will be met with tremendous apprehension from students who are appropriately fearful of confessing desires and putting their lives on display for academic scrutiny. While such realities should not dissuade us from engaging in pedagogies about hip-hop, they should shape the ethic of care and intellectual attentiveness that governs our practice.

PEDAGOGIES *WITH* HIP-HOP

As discussed in Chapter Two, the Hip-Hop Lit curriculum was undergirded by a belief that hip-hop culture could be effectively used to enhance student learning. While beyond the scope of this book, there remains a need to develop and articulate concrete processes for using hip-hop texts to enhance student motivation, transmit subject area knowledge, and develop habits of mind appropriate for learning. These processes, which I refer to as *pedagogies with hip-hop*, are central to the development of a hip-hop pedagogy. To be clear, I am not suggesting a rigid set of strategies or curricula to be transmitted and replicated. Such an approach only intensifies the de-skilling efforts of contemporary educational power brokers who offer prepackaged (in some cases even scripted) curricula in place of engaged, reflective, and context-specific pedagogy. Rather, I am suggesting that hip-hop–based educators and scholars move beyond esoteric theory and romantic classroom anecdotes in order to develop a vision of hip-hop pedagogy that takes seriously the importance of academic achievement.

In order to engage pedagogies with hip-hop, educators must identify how hip-hop texts can be used to navigate traditional academic subject matter. While the fields of literacy and English education have produced a sizeable amount of research in this area, there remains a need to link hip-hop to other subject areas such as mathematics, social studies, and health education. To do this, educators must draw not only from rap lyrics, but from the entire range of cultural texts produced within hip-hop culture, as well as from the unique relationships that students forge with them. How can the act of "counting bars" when writing a rap song be used to teach algebra? How could "Police State" by dead prez enable a conversation about structural inequality? How might an analysis of hip-hop "beefs" help with conflict resolution? Such possibilities, and countless others, speak to the fecund nature of hip-hop as a space for improving learning outcomes.

When designing the Hip-Hop Lit course, Mr. Colombo and I made a deliberate decision to discard traditional canonical texts and replace them with hip-hop texts in order to attract and engage the students. Despite our success, it is important not to romanticize the use of hip-hop texts. By relying on nontraditional instead of canonical texts, we deprived students of access to bodies of knowledge (in this case, knowledge of the Western literary canon) that are crucial to mainstream educational success vis-à-vis high-stakes tests and enhanced cultural capital. On its own, this type of practice can enable social reproduction by preventing students from accessing what Delpit (1995) calls the "culture of power." In this case, however, students in Hip-Hop Lit developed a formal vocabulary of literary critique that would be of considerable value within a mainstream literature classroom. Nevertheless, the tension between challenging school-sanctioned knowledge and providing students with bodies of knowledge that are requisite for mainstream educational success is one that must be carefully negotiated by hip-hop–based educators.

While the use of hip-hop texts for scaffolding purposes is significant, particularly in light of the current demands for "measurable outcomes," pedagogies of hip-hop must also locate new sites of educational possibility within hip-hop–based classrooms. In addition to using hip-hop as a scaffold for teaching traditional skills, educators must also draw from the alternative forms of knowledge and new categories of meaning that are produced through a pedagogical engagement with hip-hop culture. How does a conversation about sampling reshape how schools negotiate issues of citation and plagiarism? How do the literacies of hip-hop authorship expand traditional notions of literary analysis and canonicity? How could the notion of a "hip-hop cipher," which marks the democratic ethos of hip-hop culture, allow us to reimagine classroom participation? These examples, and the fundamental ideas that underpin them, speak to the ways in which the distinct aspects of hip-hop can contribute to a more expansive and rich intellectual space.

In order to successfully engage pedagogies with hip-hop, educators must pay careful attention to students and the cultural landscapes that they occupy. This requires a deep engagement with the aforementioned pedagogies *of* and *about* hip-hop, as well as a reflective engagement with our own practice. Following the lead of practitioner-inquiry scholars (e.g., Cochran-Smith & Lytle, 1993, 2004), hip-hop–based educators must use rigorous research methodologies in order to reflect upon and improve their own practices. In addition to determining whether or not a hip-hop–based project "worked," teachers must also raise critical questions about its dynamics: How is success being defined? Why was this project (un)successful? How is the classroom context reshaped by this project? In what ways were people (dis)empowered? What was the relationship between my own positionality and the project? What lessons does the project offer for future practice? Such questions enable hip-hop–based educators to operate as engaged teacher-researchers and critical public intellectuals.

Throughout this book, Mr. Colombo has been represented as an outsider to the Hip-Hop Lit community. Despite the temptation to dismiss his story as a narrative of failure, we must take seriously its instructive dimensions. In many ways, Mr. Colombo's marginalization and occasional disinterest foreshadows some of the challenges that many educators will face when engaging in pedagogies with hip-hop. Given the often-sharp contrasts between urban teachers and students with regard to race, gender, and class, pedagogies with hip-hop will frequently produce feelings of discomfort, alienation, and frustration. Even for educators such as myself who claim "insider" status, such feelings are an inevitable part of the pedagogical process. In order to move beyond these feelings, hip-hop–based educators must take up the ethnographic task of "making the strange familiar" and "making the familiar strange." By abandoning our teacherly positions of comfort, power, and privilege and rendering ourselves open-minded and vulnerable, we will be better equipped to take full advantage of hip-hop culture's rich rhymes and reasons.

APPENDIX

IIIIIIIIIIIIIIIIIIIIIIIIIIIIIIIIIIIIIIIIIIIIIIIIIIIIIIIIIIIIIIIIIIIIIIIIIIIIIIIIIIIIIIIIIIIIIIIIIIIIIIIII

Bonus Track

Representin(g): Negotiating Identities in the Field and Behind the Desk

"Who was I for them?"
—Jean Paul Dumont, *The Headman and I*

"What's wild now is that they smaller and they look at me like I'm on the outside lookin' in like 'Who's you?' when I cruise through."
—Nas, "Nothing Lasts Forever"

Late in the school year, after teaching the day's lesson, I asked the students to work in groups in order to complete an assignment. As the students stood up and began dividing into their groups, Dorene, one of the students in Hip-Hop Lit, made a comment that I found noteworthy and I took a free moment to write it down in my notebook. As I was writing, I could feel Joe, who had carefully watched the entire scene unfold, staring at me intensely. When I looked up from my notebook and met his eyes, he looked away with deliberate speed and genuine disgust. A few minutes later, I overheard him saying to no one in particular, "They come in and they look at us and ask us all these questions and then they bounce. They don't never tell us why they doin' it or nothin'. It's like they think we rats or monkeys or somethin'!"

Nearly a year after completing my fieldwork, I was in the process of revising Chapter Four of this book. While reading the comments that my advisor had written on a draft, I came across a question that she had placed on the margins of the page in response to a comment that I made about Mr. Colombo being "vacant." She asked, "Do you mean to diss him this much?" I reread each chapter of the book in search of the types of descriptions of Mr. Colombo that prompted her question. After reading them, I recognized a pattern within the data with regard to my descriptions of Mr. Colombo. In nearly every instance where

I had mentioned him, he was either an insignificant character or the object of veiled or explicit critique.

These two instances provided necessary "speed bumps" (Weis & Fine, 2000), or moments in the research where I was forced to pause and reflect on the methodological and ethical concerns that inform the development of this study. Up to the point of my encounter with Joe, I had not interrogated or even acknowledged the various and often contradictory ways that I was positioned within HHS. Instead, as a former teacher at the school (and of several of the students in the class), I had presumed that I held the unique and privileged position of being a legitimate insider who could merely deploy rigorous ethnographic methods in order to enrich my research and make "the familiar strange." In this case, despite my best intentions and efforts, I had somehow become or remained part of the "they" instead of the "we" to whom Joe referred. In the second instance, my advisor's comments forced me to reflect on the impact of my writing in presenting Mr. Colombo to the world. To this point, I had not seriously reflected upon the motivations and ramifications of choosing the particular words, descriptions, and stories that represent him and the other people within this text.

These two instances thus served as jarring notices that my roles within this research study were far different and more complicated than I had imagined. From these points forward, I began to think critically about how I was positioned within the study in relation to the research participants: Who was I to them? Who was I for them? Who did I want to be to them? I also began to consider how such considerations extend beyond the field and into the process of writing this study: What stories should I tell? How did I want readers to see them? How did I want readers to see me? Each of these questions, along with myriad others, points to the significance of various forms of representation that I have been engaged in from the moment this book was conceived in my mind until the time that it reaches the reader's eyes. Such questions push this chapter beyond a closer analysis or retrospective assessment of the research methods that have been deployed in this study. Rather, they link methodological reflection to the book's broader themes of authenticity, storytelling, and identity formation.

In this chapter, I draw from a concept that I refer to as "representin(g)" in order to examine how my identity in the field as co-teacher, researcher, and mentor was mediated by the various allegiances, commitments, and beliefs that prompted the study, as well as those that developed in response to the relationships that I forged with the members of the research community. I also look at how the challenges of representin(g) extended beyond fieldwork and into the practice of writing, where I encountered equally formidable dilemmas and tensions regarding the particular stories from the field that I constructed "behind the desk."

REPRESENTIN(G)

This chapter is theoretically undergirded by a concept that I call *representin(g)*. With this term, I mean to illumine the various ways that my relationship to the research context was mediated by my own struggles to negotiate the multiple forms of representation that my roles as co-teacher, researcher, and mentor demanded. I make parenthetical use of the letter "g" in representin*(g)* in order to acknowledge the tensions that necessarily emerged as I tried to simultaneously engage in forms of "representing" and "representin'" within this study. I use the term "representing" in acknowledgment of the ways that my research shares in the ethnographic tradition of attempting, to varying degrees of success, to conduct research that accurately reflects the "realities" of a cultural space through participant-observation. I borrow "representin'" from the vernacular of hip-hop culture, where it speaks to the political dimensions of "authentic" representation within the hip-hop and broader African American communities, in order to highlight the relationship between my personal allegiances and commitments and my roles and functions within this study.

Representing

The issue of representing lies at the heart of the ethnographic project. While severely undermined by questionable identity politics, representation has nonetheless been the telos of the ethnographic enterprise, with each epistemological and methodological turn being offered with the goal of providing a more full and accurate depiction of a culture. Nevertheless, due to its long history of methodological, epistemological, and ethical shortcomings, ethnographic work has been long implicated in the maintenance of the imperial project due to its fetishization of the exotic and problematic constructions of the "Other" (Hymes, 1972; Pratt, 1986; Said, 1979) in its textual representations. Beginning with the late-19th-century anthropological work of the "lone ethnographer" (Kamberelis & Dimitriadis, 2005; Rosaldo,

1989), ethnographic fieldwork and writing have been consistently marred by inattentiveness to the ways that human subjectivity is concealed within its texts.

Over the past 20 years, ethnographers have devoted significant scholarly attention to responding to the field's failure to account for the ways that the researcher's subject position directly informs the collection, analysis, and writing of fieldwork and the construction of culture. As Dimitriadis (1999) notes, there have been several significant scholarly responses to this "crisis of representation" (Clifford, 1988; Clifford & Marcus, 1986), including experimentation with alternate forms of representation, giving more autonomy to the voices of the subject, researching the self, and "interrogat[ing] the line between self and other" (p. 39). These decolonizing gestures index an "end to innocence" (Maanen, 1995) in ethnographic practice and the development of a more nuanced understanding of the ways that the ethnographer is at once observing and constituting culture.

As many scholars (Clifford, 1986; Dimitriadis, 1999; Richardson, 2000) have noted, the power of ethnography to constitute culture is not exhausted at the level of fieldwork. Rather, the choice of genre, style, metaphor, or format within ethnographic writing all help to constitute the particular narratives that emerge from behind the ethnographer's desk. For example, Richardson (2000) demonstrates how the metaphor of "the building," through words like "structure," "grand," "framework," and "construction," pervades social science writing. It is through these arbitrarily (though certainly not randomly) selected methods for ethnographic writing that we create and delimit possibilities for analyzing particular phenomena.

Representin'

The term "representin'" comes from the vernacular of hip-hop culture and African American public life more broadly, where it is used in several interrelated ways. For example, a brief review of several major magazines (*Source*, *Ebony*, and *XXL*) yielded the following results: the graffiti artist who spray-paints the name of her neighborhood on public walls is said to be "representin' their block"; the poor African American student who succeeds in college and attains social mobility is charged with "representin' for the community"; the rap artist whose lyrics describe the quotidian dimensions of postindustrial urban spaces is said to be "representin' the hood."

In each of these examples, representin' refers to the practice of sustaining allegiances to community and meeting locally constructed standards of authenticity. Within the hip-hop context, "representin'" means sustaining one's commitment to particular social practices and forms of representation that honor the values, experiences, and truths of home regardless of geographic location or economic position. Within the broader context of African American public life from which the notion of representin' is conceived, the burdens of representation require an individual to function in ways that benefit the community to which she is inexorably linked. Like the conception of realness discussed in detail in Chapter Three, representin' requires a commitment not only to authenticity, but to particular articulations of authenticity that frequently underwrite various forms of essentialism, parochialism, and insularity (Dyson, 1993; West, 1993). This book is largely informed by the notion of representin', as it is shaped by the particular beliefs, experiences, and allegiances that prompted its conception (see Chapter One), development, and ultimate completion.

Representin(g)

The concept of representin(g) thus reflects the tension that appears as I attempt to engage in complex and reflexive forms of ethnographic representation while simultaneously sustaining authentic and organic links to particular physical and imagined communities. Representin(g) is about more than who the researcher purports herself and her research participants to be, i.e., Who am I? Who are they? Representin(g) is also about the complicated phenomenological processes that a researcher negotiates while "working the hyphens" (Fine, 1994), or negotiating the complex relationships between the researcher and the multiple roles and contexts in which they operate in order to resist the practice of "othering" research participants. When representin(g) within a particular space, the researcher must consistently ask, to borrow from Ellsworth's (1997) work on modes of address within the practice of teaching, "Who do they think that I am?" But also, "Who do I think I am?," "Who do I want them to think that I am?," and "Who do I want people to think that they are?" Such questions reflect the importance of "working the hyphens," but also demand a closer and more deliberate analysis of the experiences, beliefs, allegiances, and commitments that shape who and how the researcher writes into existence. Additionally, unlike "working the hyphen," which focuses primarily on the reflexive dimensions of ethnographic work in process, representin(g) also calls for a retrospective analysis of the work that is done in the field and behind the desk. In the remainder of the chapter, I draw from new and revisited data in order to critically examine the ways that I am representin(g) throughout this study.

WHO YOU WIT'?: REPRESENTIN(G) IN THE FIELD

Although I was not always reflexive enough throughout the study to ask myself critical questions about who I was in relation to the research participants, I nonetheless made decisions about how I wanted to represent myself in my various roles as teacher, researcher, and mentor within this study. These decisions largely informed the way that the various members of the Hip-Hop Lit and larger HHS communities saw me, thereby creating and eliminating possibilities for the types of research, teaching, and mentoring that I could engage in within the research context.

Representin(g) as Teacher

Although I fully expected to conduct rigorous research when I arrived at HHS, I also relished my role as a teacher within the project. As a former teacher at the school and a full-time graduate student, I was excited by the prospect of being a high school teacher again. Although I did not regret my decision to leave HHS and attend graduate school, I still felt a sense of guilt for leaving the students to pursue my personal goals. Not only did I miss the day-to-day interactions with students, but I also looked forward to applying many of the theoretical insights that I had gained from graduate school in an actual classroom.

In addition to satisfying my desire to return to the classroom, I also believed that my hands-on participation within the school as a teacher would bolster my credibility among the large number of HHS students, teachers, and administrators who were both weary and wary of the presence of researchers in the school. Much of this tension surrounding research was a response to the increasing levels and forms of surveillance that accompanied the growing amount of high-stakes testing within the school. Also, many people in the school were simply tired of researchers who, as Mr. Ormond described, "come in and do their work and leave without giving anything back" (interview, 5/12/03). Consequently, to draw from Chapter Three's discussion of authenticity politics, I felt a sense that being a researcher was not a "real" enough role within the school to allow me access into the very social networks that I would need in order to conduct "real" research.

For these reasons, I went out of my way to demonstrate that I was giving back throughout the year by serving as an unpaid substitute teacher, staying late to help Mr. Ormond perform administrative work, and chaperoning student events. I rarely spoke about my presence in the school as being part of a research project, preferring instead to tell people that I had returned to the school to teach a hip-hop class. For this reason, most of the teachers and students outside Hip-Hop Lit did not know that I was not employed by the school as an official teacher. In fact, Mr. Ormond approached me in late December to tell me that several teachers had complained to the administration that he had violated union regulations by "hiring" me without following appropriate district procedures.

Many of the students thought that I was not only an official teacher, but also the lead teacher in my co-teaching relationship with Mr. Colombo. This became apparent to me the first day that Mr. Colombo was absent and a student asked me without sarcasm where my "assistant" was. When I responded that Mr. Colombo was an equal partner and the only one of us who was actually paid to teach the class, most of the students expressed genuine surprise. Although several of the teachers and a few of the students in the school were friends and former colleagues who knew that I was conducting graduate school research, I would typically minimize the importance of the research in our conversations by describing it as something that I had to do in order to justify teaching the course. In sum, I attempted to present myself as a teacher whose research was incidental to the more legitimate classroom work that was being done.

By establishing myself as a "real" teacher, I was able to develop relationships with other teachers in the school that would likely have been extremely limited or entirely unavailable to me as a researcher. Insider advantages such as teachers-only meetings, hallway gossip circles, and warnings of upcoming surprise teacher evaluations were all accessible for me largely because the teachers in the school did not view me as a researcher. This point was made clearer to me as I was sitting in the classroom of Mr. Rogers, a Twilight teacher with whom I had no prior relationship as a colleague or friend, talking about his impressions of the Twilight program. In the middle of our conversation, a graduate student from a nearby university entered the class and asked Mr. Rogers when he would be free to talk about the upcoming math assessment tests. Mr. Rogers responded by telling her that he was extremely busy and would get back to him as soon as he could. After the graduate student left, Mr. Rogers apologized for the interruption and added, "those damn people from [the university] are always coming in here and interrupting us." When I pointed out that I was both from a university and conducting research, he laughed and replied, "Oh yeah! But you're different. You're one of us." Such comments were typical throughout the year and reflected the sense of belonging that many of the teachers in the school enabled me to feel throughout the school year.

While my level of "insiderness" in many ways reflects the appropriate application of ethnographic methods (gaining entry, developing rapport, etc.), it also limited the types of interactions that I was able to have with teachers at HHS. For example, when conducting interviews with other teachers, the conversations would often lose focus, turning into gossip sessions or complaints about the school. Also, it became increasingly difficult to get the teachers to take time after or before school to talk to me or to provide other information. When I complained about this to Mr. Ormond, he gave me the following insight:

> You know, Marc. Most of the time I forget that you're here
> doing research. . . . I mean it's good because it means that we're
> comfortable with you, you're one of us. But I know it's hard for
> you because. . . . Take me for example. I know at the beginning
> when you got here, I would go out of my way to meet and
> talk to you and find stuff for you and answer your questions.
> Now sometimes I say, "Why can't he do it himself?" [laughing]
> I mean, I catch myself and remember that you're still a guest
> in here but I know it's even harder for the other teachers. I'm
> guessing to them you were like a new teacher and now you
> should know better.

Mr. Ormond's observation speaks to the underside of representin(g) as a teacher within HHS. As a "real" teacher I was afforded numerous advantages in terms of access, support, and personal reward. But because I was no longer an exotic researcher, I was also denied the special treatment that is often awarded to outsiders.

The high level of access that was facilitated through the teachers' failure to recognize my "undercover" status also created ethical dilemmas that were difficult to resolve. One such dilemma emerged toward the middle of the school year as I began to sit in the teachers' lounge before the beginning of the HHSTP school day, during the midevening break, as well as other moments when the students were not in class. During this time, I would frequently engage in conversations with the day school and HHSTP teachers, who would often make disparaging off-the-record comments about the students, administrators, and other teachers at HHS, as well as share extremely personal stories without any regard for my presence in the room. For HHSTP teachers, their candor was largely because of my successful performance of teacher identity such that they forgot or ignored the fact that I was a researcher. With respect to the day school teachers, however, many of whom I had not formally met, there seemed to be a basic assumption that I was a teacher.

Although I did not find my presence in the room to be fundamentally problematic—I had no intentions of misusing the information that was offered in the teachers' lounge—I understood that the lounge was a place reserved exclusively for teachers. No one at HHS, including administrators, was permitted inside the lounge except for teachers. Consequently, I worried about the ethicality of passively confirming the entirely reasonable assumption that I was "one of them" through my somewhat deliberate silence. Although I technically was a teacher in the program and could therefore mount a reasonable defense if I were "outed" as a researcher, I knew that the teachers likely would not have been as open with me in the room if they had fully understood my role at HHS. After recognizing my dilemma, I considered introducing myself to everyone in the lounge. I worried, however, that such an act would undermine my successful entry into the school. Instead, I decided not to sit in the teachers' lounge anymore and began to stay in Mr. Colombo's and my classroom during down times.

Representin(g) as a Researcher

Despite my efforts to represent myself to the HHS community as a "real" teacher who simply happened to be conducting research, I frequently did the opposite in my interactions with Mr. Colombo. Throughout the school year, I consistently represented myself to him as a researcher and academic for whom teaching was of secondary or incidental importance. Although my actions were not always intentional, they nonetheless created many tensions in our relationship that ultimately complicated the way that I conducted research and co-taught the class.

At times, I made deliberate decisions to represent myself as a researcher to provide intellectual direction and leadership for the project. For example, before our first curriculum meeting, I asked Mr. Colombo to read a draft of an article that I was preparing to submit to an academic journal on hip-hop literacy and pedagogy, as well as a few other academic articles, so that he could obtain a better understanding of my perspectives on hip-hop culture and my vision for a hip-hop–centered English course. Although he admittedly never read any of the articles, always saying that he was too busy but would eventually get around to it, I continued to make references to academic figures and theories. Also, I would begin many of my statements with comments such as "In the field . . ."as a way of reiterating the academic underpinnings (and consequent legitimacy) of our project.

In addition to facilitating our curricular goals, a (perhaps more important) reason for representin(g) as a researcher to Mr. Colombo was my own defensiveness about the legitimacy of my work, as well as academic research in general, in my encounters with him. This was because of the fact that Mr. Colombo, who himself held a master's degree in English education, would often joke with me about the nature and rigor of my academic interests in hip-hop literacy and pedagogy. He would also make more generally disparaging remarks about academics who, as he once said to me, "think of really silly stuff and make it seem deep." Although he was always careful to offer his comments in jest, I nonetheless felt that he did not take my intellectual interests and work seriously from the onset of the project. For this reason, I wanted to show Mr. Colombo that my decision to leave the classroom to pursue graduate study was a worthwhile one—this desire was also linked to my guilt about leaving the classroom—as I had become a "real" researcher who was doing "real" work during my time away.

Although I often tried to follow Mr. Colombo's cues and refrain from formally invoking academic texts within our project development, there were other ways that I represented myself as a researcher that were unintentional and became apparent only in immediate retrospect or during formal data analysis. These acts contributed greatly to how Mr. Colombo saw me, as well as his own role within the classroom and the overall project. One of the major ways that this occurred was through my persistent use of academic language in my interactions with Mr. Colombo. The following vignette, taken from our first curriculum meeting, illustrates how my decision to represent myself through academic language within our interactions frequently discomforted and alienated Mr. Colombo. In this exchange, Mr. Colombo and I are beginning our first conversation about the structure of Hip-Hop Lit:

> *Me*: We need to find a way to organize the class by beginning with central texts and letting the students . . .
> *Colombo*: I thought we were using songs.
> *Me*: We are, but . . .
> *Colombo*: But we're writing them down.
> *Me*: That too, but when I talk about text I'm talking about various things like TV, video, . . .
> *Colombo*: So it's *not* text.
> *Me*: Well, I use a more expansive notion of text . . . [pause] kinda postmodern.
> *Colombo*: What's postmodern?
> *Me*: Well, for *this* it's a way of looking at multiple kinds of text and challenging interpretations.
> *Colombo*: Whatever. What's next?
> *Me*: Well, I wanted to think of what kinds of texts to use.
> *Colombo*: Well?
> *Me*: What do you think?
> *Colombo*: I think whatever you think. This is your kid. I'm just babysittin'.

In this exchange, what began as an ostensibly democratic dialogue quickly degenerated into a conversation that effectively silenced Mr. Colombo. What I considered to be a clear and innocuous use of the term *text* triggered a highly complicated and significant exchange that ultimately privileged academic language at the expense of Mr. Colombo's comfort and usefulness within the meeting.

Despite my explicit and implicit arguments to the contrary, the pervasiveness of academic discourse within our interactions was not a necessary evil. As a former teacher at HHS and a friend of Mr. Colombo, I was certainly capable of engaging in less formal and ultimately more productive conversations with him. In fact, several of the teachers expressed comments similar to Mr. Rogers, who said that I "get a lot of respect around here because you don't talk down to us," or presumably rely on the type of language that I used in my interactions with Mr. Colombo. Nevertheless, I consistently made decisions that allowed me to be a researcher and not a teacher in my interactions with Mr. Colombo, despite the clear ineffectiveness of such a move. These decisions ultimately contributed to the asymmetric power relationship that developed between Mr. Colombo and me that ultimately led him to consider the class to be "my kid" that he was merely "babysitting."

Representin(g) as Mentor and Friend

In addition to my roles as teacher and researcher, I served as a mentor and friend to many of the students in Hip-Hop Lit. At various points throughout this study, this role forced me to protect the interests of the students and privilege my relationships with them in ways that enriched particular portions of the study and compromised others. Moreover, my role as mentor and friend to the students further complicated my professional and personal relationship with Mr. Colombo. Although I imagined that the roles of teacher and researcher would be critical to this study from the onset, the role of mentor emerged rather unexpectedly throughout the school year. One of the reasons that I became a mentor to many of the students in Hip-Hop Lit was because of my previous position as a teacher at the school. Many of the students were former day school attendees who had taken one of my classes or had other in-school contact with me. Through these interactions, I had already forged many close relationships with the students.

Another thing that contributed to the development of my relationships with many of the students was the practice of storytelling that frequently took place in the class. The members of Hip-Hop Lit would often share personal narratives that facilitated the development of a cohesive classroom community and many out-of-school relationships. Like many of the students in the class, I began to develop closer in-school and out-of-school relationships with particular students as my acts of personal disclosure increased throughout the school year. For example, after a conversation about "baby mommas" (unmarried female co-parents) during the Family unit, Hakeem and I began to speak more regularly outside of the classroom about various aspects of our personal lives. Toward the end of the school year, I would often give him a ride home and provide him with advice about various issues that he wanted to discuss. Also, my connection to Supreme, as detailed elsewhere (Hill, 2005), was largely because of my willingness to share with him my own experiences with the particular Afrocentric books and cultural spaces that he was navigating. For this reason, and because Supreme rarely came to school, our relationship extended beyond the classroom and persists even at the time of this writing. Through these types of interactions, I developed bonds with many of the students that positioned me as their mentor and friend within various spaces.

As an ethnographer, my role as mentor and friend to the students of Hip-Hop Lit was extremely beneficial, as it provided me with access to parts of the students' lives that would have otherwise been unavailable to me. For example, much of my data on Supreme come from my out-of-school experiences with him as a friend and mentor. Without such experiences, I would have been unable to fully understand the personal resonances of particular Afrocentric texts in relationship to his developing Afrocentric identity (Hill, 2005). Such relationships were extremely fruitful, as they enabled me to develop the research while providing the students with what I considered to be much-needed guidance and support.

Although helpful, my role as friend and mentor also created ethical challenges for me as I reached points throughout the research where I felt that I had to choose between doing good ethnography and being a good friend and mentor. For example, nearly 2 weeks after Supreme and I began to talk regularly, he called me and asked if we could meet downtown at a restaurant to talk. Soon after I arrived, the conversation took a serious turn as Supreme began to share extremely personal information with me. I nodded empathetically and offered honest and careful responses as he began to tell me stories about his father in prison, his quest for knowledge, and his struggles with personal identity. As he continued to talk, my mind was soon doing the double duty of processing his stories and thinking about ways to connect his stories to the themes that were developing in my research. Suddenly worried about losing "good data," I asked Supreme if he would mind if I "took a few notes from time to time." Although Supreme told me that he did not mind my note-taking, his suddenly despondent tone and awkward body language suggested that my request shifted the nature of the interaction from friendly conversation to informal interview. He soon changed the subject and began to talk about something less personal. Although our conversations eventually regained their prior level of depth and disclosure, several meetings passed in which I felt that Supreme was being guarded and defensive. From that point on, I rarely used a tape recorder or took detailed notes in front of Supreme, usually opting to go into a nearby bathroom or empty classroom and quickly empty the contents of my mind onto a piece of notepaper that I had stuffed into one of my pants pockets.

This example illustrates more than bad methodology or poor social skills, although it shows both quite lucidly. Rather, it also speaks directly to the tensions inherent in engaging in research about people with whom one has developed personal relationships. As discussed in the previous section, the researcher must ask at critical junctures within the research project, "Who do I want to be?" and "Who do I want to be *to them*?" From this analytic posture, it becomes clear that even if I had not changed the tenor of the conversation by asking if I could take notes, I would have still been misrepresenting myself as a friend and mentor while literally thinking like a researcher. This became more apparent to me during a conversation that occurred between Supreme and me as I was in the process of writing this chapter.

As I was working on this section of the chapter, I began wondering if Supreme would agree with my assessment about the dilemmas of being a researcher and friend with respect to his and my relationship. I called him and asked if he felt that I was really a friend to him or if I was simply trying to do research. After a thoughtful pause, he offered the following:

> I'm sayin', Hill, sometimes when we rappin' it's like you just my oldhead and we rappin' and then sometime it's like you on the job, y'ah mean. I mean, your job is tight anyway so it's all good but I just used to be wonderin' if you be asking shit 'cause you wanted to know or if you was askin' so that you would have a good story.

Although I am unsure if it was his intention, the poignancy of Supreme's comment and the accompanying irony were not lost on me. My primary reason for calling Supreme and asking him how he viewed me was not to ensure that we had a healthy friendship mediated by mutual respect but rather to triangulate my data through an informal interview. I was doing the very thing about which he was expressing concern. I suddenly felt like an imposter who was merely posing as a mentor to enrich my research.

This incident reveals how my role as a researcher often coerced me into stretching and even exceeding the ethical bounds of my role as friend and vice versa. Although Supreme was fully aware that I was a researcher who was conducting research, our relationship clearly extended beyond the boundaries of the researcher–researched binary. Consequently, I often found myself in the ignoble paradox of choosing between doing good research and dishonoring the relationships that I developed, or between being a good friend and failing to execute a rigorous ethnographic study.

Although it can be argued that such dilemmas can be and in fact were resolved through more creative research methods—in this case taking furtive notes outside Supreme's purview—such moves fail to address the more fundamental ethical questions that were raised as I was representin(g) myself as a mentor and friend to Supreme: Who did I want to be in my relationship with Supreme? Who do I want Supreme to think that I was in our relationship? In responding to these questions in the way that I did, by offering myself as a friend and mentor and secretly functioning like a researcher, I created a contradiction between who I was and who I wanted Supreme to think that I was. Although Supreme was keenly aware of this, as evidenced by his comments, it did not relieve the ethical weight attached to the particular ways that I represented and failed to represent for Supreme in our relationship and in my research.

My relationship with many of the students in Hip-Hop Lit also created noticeable tension between Mr. Colombo and me that affected the way that we taught the class. Within Hip-Hop Lit, there was a sense that the students' and my relationship was superordinate to the relationship between Mr. Colombo and me, as well as the relationship between Mr. Colombo and the students. This was pointed out to me by Mr. Colombo himself at the end of a class session in which a student offered me a piece of his sandwich but denied Mr. Colombo's playful request for the same. He offered, "I know the students like you better than me and that's okay, I guess. But sometimes I don't know what to say to them because it's like they're *your* kids, not mine." Although the truth of Mr. Colombo's comments can be largely attributed to my relationships with the students, it is also because of Mr. Colombo's failure to fully involve himself in the classroom community. Mr. Colombo's tendency to listen but not share contributed to his position outside of the "real" classroom community. As Jay explained later in the year,

"It's like it's us against him. Not on no hostile shit, y'ah mean. He cool and everything but, like, he a outsider to our family."

The sentiment that Mr. Colombo and Jay expressed became increasingly obvious throughout the year, as the students would often come to me to complain about Mr. Colombo. I further enabled this behavior by encouraging the students to talk about Mr. Colombo to me when he was absent from school. During these conversations, none of the students expressed any concern about discussing Mr. Colombo while he was not in class. On the contrary, students would frequently report to me that Mr. Colombo was "behind my back" on days that I was absent. Although the comments attributed to him were rarely mean-spirited or in my mind noteworthy, they further demonstrate the students' allegiance to me in relation to Mr. Colombo. Although my primary reason for having the "behind-the-back" conversations was to enrich my data, they also helped to created the "us against him" feeling that pervaded the classroom.

WHAT STORIES DO I TELL?:
REPRESENTIN(G) BEHIND THE DESK

The challenges of representin(g) extended beyond my work in the field and into the process of writing this study. One of the fundamental challenges that I faced behind the desk was deciding how to construct a rigorous ethnography that honored the relationships that I had developed in the field. Specifically, I struggled with the responsibility of deciding which stories were suitable to include within this text. In this section, I examine some of the tensions that emerged as I attempted to represent the research participants from behind the desk.

Telling Tales Out of School

One of the most significant features of Hip-Hop Lit was its focus on individual and collective storytelling through the practice of wounded healing. While the Hip-Hop Lit classroom functioned as a space in which each participant elected to expose their own personal and ideological wounds at the moment that they deemed appropriate, the responsibility of deciding which of these wounds would be included within the text of this study was solely mine once behind the desk. While the most primary concerns about protecting the identity of the research participants could be addressed through the pro forma ethnographic practice of giving pseudonyms to the research participants, a more complicated issue persisted around the act of "telling tales out of school," or repeating stories outside of their appropriate context (Rogers, 1986). The expression, which typically alludes to gossip or other forms of inappropriate storytelling, reflects my worries about sharing the stories of Hip-Hop Lit with outsiders.

Although I navigated the traditional rituals of formal data analysis (looking for patterns in the data, identifying discrepant cases, etc.) rather comfortably, I encountered a feeling of enormous dissonance as I began to craft the actual narrative of this study. Specifically, I found it extremely difficult to "expose the wounds" of the students in Hip-Hop Lit to potential readers of this study and subsequent texts (journal articles, books, etc.) that would rely on their stories as data. As I wrote, I encountered new "speed bumps" as I began to wonder, "What would the students want me to write?" and "What would they want the world to know about them?" Such questions suggested to me that my obligations to the members of Hip-Hop Lit and to the spirit of our community could not be fulfilled by rendering pseudonymous the people whose stories, experiences, and practices constructed and sustained the community and constituted my research. Instead, I engaged in a closer examination of how I was representin(g) their stories within the body of this text.

Although all of the students in Hip-Hop Lit were completely aware that I was conducting a research study and consented to full participation before enrolling in the course, most did so early in the semester before the practice of wounded healing took full form. This point is critical because, as discussed in Chapter Four, most of the students entered the class with expectations similar to Dorene, who noted that she "wasn't gonna say nothin' if ain't nobody else say nothin'." Consequently, the link between personal disclosure and participation in the study was not necessarily clear at the onset to everyone involved in Hip-Hop Lit.

This is not to suggest that the students were unaware of the nature of the research or the fact that they were sharing stories that would eventually be used as data. In fact, both Mr. Colombo and I reiterated the nature of the project at numerous points throughout the semester. Moreover, as Supreme's previous comment about me "looking for a good story" suggests, the students were keenly aware of and deliberate about the types of stories that they were offering within the class.

Nevertheless, as students began to participate to varying degrees in the practice of wounded healing and other personal forms of storytelling, there were multiple instances where they became immersed in the conversation and lost sight of the fact that their words would likely be taken up by people outside the class. This point was reinforced by Josh, who told me the following in response to my question about the presence of the tape recorder in the class:

> It didn't even matter most of the time. I knew you was tapin' everything. . . . I mean the camera was right there. But still, sometime you get so caught up in what you sayin' that it don't even matter. Then you be walkin' home or whatever and you be like, "shit, he got that on tape."

The tendency to get caught up in the moment and let one's guard down during storytelling was not restricted to the students. A few days after talking to the students about my worries surrounding my unexpected child and potential "baby momma" problems, I began to worry that I had disclosed too much information to the students.

Although I eventually concluded that I had done the appropriate thing by sharing my story with the class, similar worries appeared as I was writing about the experience in Chapter Four. I began to consider the consequences of exposing myself within the text and wondered, "Do I want to share this part of my life with the readers?" Again, I eventually decided that it was important to include this narrative within the text in order to accurately represent the practices of Hip-Hop Lit and to render myself as textually vulnerable (at least for that particular moment) as the other research participants. Nevertheless, the fact that I had a second chance, an opportunity to re-present myself within the text by omitting or including particular stories, and the other research participants did not, speaks directly to a critical challenge of representin(g) from behind the desk. The story of Keneka provides an excellent example of how I negotiated this challenge.

One of the major dilemmas that I confronted behind the desk came as I was writing about Keneka and my interactions surrounding our reading of the abortion texts mentioned in Chapter Four. As I was writing the story, I suddenly began to wonder if Keneka would approve of me including such a story within the text. After completing a draft, I gave her a copy and asked her to read it and tell me if she found it acceptable. At first, she told me that she did not approve of the text because she did not want "my business put out there like that." I reminded her that I would not be using her real name and emphasized the importance of sharing her story in order to help others. After nearly an hour of convincing, she agreed to permit me to include her story provided that I exclude several details that were in the draft that she had read.

Soon after complying with Keneka's request, I realized that the information that she wanted me to exclude was critical for an analytic point that I wanted to make in the chapter. I contacted Keneka again and reiterated the importance of including the details that she wanted excluded from the study. She refused to concede but added, "I don't know why you asking. You know you gonna do it anyway!" Her comment, which I interpreted as being equal parts cynical declaration and appeal to my ethics, intensified my ambivalence about the issue. While I sincerely believe that the included information was completely within the ethical boundaries of ethnographic research, I also shared Keneka's belief that it was still "her business" regardless of the pseudonym that I superimposed over her name and despite the fact that I had the unilateral power to include or exclude the information. After a week of deliberation, I ultimately decided to exclude the information. Although I sacrificed a small bit of analytic rigor from this study, I was able to honor the spirit of Keneka and my relationship and continue representin(g) for her behind the desk.

Airing Dirty Laundry

While concerns about telling tales out of school have a deep history within American society, they have particular significance within the African American community, where the concept refers not only to the practice of revealing personal stories, but also the historically taboo practice of "airing dirty laundry" (Dyson, 2005; McWhorter, 2001), or speaking publicly about the negative cultural dimensions of the community. For African Americans, telling unflattering stories about themselves is highly problematic due to their potential appropriation and misuse within a racist American context (Dyson, 2005). For example, in 2004 comedian and philanthropist Bill Cosby was publicly criticized for his comments regarding the alleged anti-intellectualism, immorality, and laziness of the African American working poor. While some (e.g., Dyson, 2005) rightly challenged the veracity of the comments themselves, other critics expressed concern solely for the ways that such comments would be inappropriately used by the Right to further its political agenda (Farley, 2004). I experienced similar concerns as I reflected on the stories from Hip-Hop Lit that I wanted to include in the text. Unlike during my time in the field, I consistently asked myself, "Who do I want people to think they are?" while behind the desk. Consequently, I began to carefully consider the ramifications of representin(g) the students in the particular ways that I did. My work with Supreme, which is rooted in this fieldwork and written about elsewhere (Hill, 2005), provides a lucid example of this dilemma.

After writing the story of Supreme, I began to consider which details about him I should include in the text. Particularly, I wondered about the potential effects of mentioning that he was a drug dealer. Unsure, I approached Supreme and asked him if he approved of my representation of his story. Unlike Keneka, Supreme read the entire text and approved all of it, adding, "I want people to know that niggas from the 'hood is smart." As his comments suggest, Supreme had thought carefully about how his story would be taken up by potential readers and decided that it was beneficial to include such details. Nevertheless, I remained particularly protective of Supreme's identity within the text. I worried that readers would ignore the brilliance of his insights and the depths of his passion for learning in spite of an often-hostile schooling context, instead reading the text as yet another public narrative about ostensibly disaffected youth. I felt similar concerns when deciding whether or not to highlight the students' use of African American Vernacular English, mentioning Hakeem's two children born 1 month apart, or telling the world that I was a "baby daddy." Would these narratives force readers to challenge their assumptions and beliefs about us, or would they cause them to dismiss us *a priori* because of them? Was I instigating social change or enabling voyeurism?

Following the advice of Supreme, I decided to include the information about him being a drug dealer, relying upon his premise that the study would serve the purpose of unsettling majoritarian narratives about "niggas from the hood." In spite of my wariness, I also made similar decisions about most of the other stories from Hip-Hop Lit about which I was uncertain. In an effort to assuage some of my anxieties, I revisited the remainder of the text and revised significant portions of it in order to add greater complexity and nuance to my representations. For example, in other writing about Supreme (Hill, 2005), I added a sentence mentioning that Supreme goes to the bookstore twice a week in order to reinforce his genuine interest in learning. Also, when deciding between two equally appropriate and almost identical quotes to include for the section on "moral inferiority," I chose the one from Keneka in an effort to demonstrate her thoughtfulness and complexity in anticipation of stereotypical readings of pregnant African American girls.

The examples of Keneka and Supreme represent some of my more successful moments behind the desk. In each of these examples, I was able to negotiate the writing process *with* the student. For various reasons, however, I was not always able to engage in such negotiations with every person whose story is represented within this text. For this reason, as in most research projects, the majority of the decisions about representin(g) the students from behind the desk were made exclusively by me.

REPRESENTIN(G) AT THE HYPHEN

Dimitriadis (2001) has accurately noted that "there are no safe spaces, no alibis, for researchers anymore. We face *ever-present and unavoidable choices* [italics added] about our commitments to the people with whom we work, choices that have implications for all manner of ethnographic practice" (p. 595). As I have demonstrated throughout this chapter, these conscious and unconscious choices reflect the commitments, allegiances, and beliefs that unavoidably inform our negotiation of qualitative research. Moreover, the decisions that we make about how we want to represent ourselves and our research participants, both in the field and behind the desk, have powerful personal, social, and methodological implications that cannot be adequately responded to through traditional methodological considerations of validity, internal generalizability, or thick description.

To address the personal and professional dilemmas that emerge as a consequence of "coming clean at the hyphen" (Dimitriadis, 2001; Fine et al., 2000), researchers must consistently wrestle with issues of identity, authority, and power throughout their time in the field and behind the desk. As discussed earlier, this means that researchers must assume a decidedly reflexive and reflective posture that enables them to constantly (re)focus how they are representin(g) themselves and their research participants. Although this process can be facilitated through increasingly democratic and dialogical interactions with research participants (as in the above examples of Keneka and Supreme), much of the burden of representation ultimately lies with the researcher.

As such, the researcher must examine the various personal and professional stakes attached to particular ways of representin(g). Some questions that enable this type of examination are: "Who am I to them?" "Who am I for them?" "Who do I want to be to them?" "What stories do I tell?" "How do I want readers to see them?" "How do I want readers to see me?" To be sure, these questions are not exhaustive. They must be supplemented or supplanted by others that reflect the particular concerns, beliefs, commitments, and contexts of the individual researcher. Nevertheless, they provide a critical starting point from which to begin representin(g).

References

Abrahams, R. D. (1970). *Deep down in the jungle: Negro narrative folklore from the streets of Philadelphia*. Chicago: Aldine.

Abu-Lughod, L. (1990). The romance of resistance: Tracing transformations of power through Bedouin women. *American Ethnologist, 17*(1), 41–55

Adorno, T. (1998). On popular music. In J. Storey (Ed.), *Cultural theory and popular culture: A reader* (pp. 197–209). Athens: University of Georgia Press.

Adorno, T., & Horkheimer, M. (1944). *Dialectic of enlightenment.* New York: Continuum.

Alim, S. (2006). *Roc the mic right: The language of hip-hop culture*. New York: Routledge.

Alvermann, D., Moon, J., & Hagood, M. (1999). *Popular culture in the classroom: Teaching and researching critical media literacy*. Newark, DE: International Reading Association.

Anderson, E. (1999). *Code of the street*. New York: Norton.

Anderson, G. (1989). Critical ethnography in education: Origins, current status, and new directions. *Review of Educational Research, 59*(3), 249–270.

Ang, I. (1985). *Watching* Dallas*: Soap opera and the melodramatic imagination*. London: Methuen.

Appadurai, A. (1991). Global ethnoscapes: Notes and queries for a transnational anthropology. In R. Fox (Ed.), *Recapturing anthropology* (pp. 191–210). Santa Fe, NM: School of American Research Press.

Appiah, A. (1992). *In my father's house: Africa in the philosophy of culture*. New York: Oxford University Press.

Apple, M. (1993). *Official knowledge*. New York: Routledge.

Arnold, M. (1932). *Culture and anarchy*. Cambridge: Cambridge University Press.

Asante, M. K. (1991). The Afrocentric idea in education. In F. L. Hord & J. S. Lee (Eds.), *I am because we are* (pp. 338–349). Amherst: University of Massachusetts Press.

Bal, M. (1999). *Quoting Caravaggio: Contemporary art, preposterous history*. Chicago: University of Chicago Press.

Barclay, C. R. (1988). Schematization of autobiographical memory. In D. C. Rubin (Ed.), *Autobiographical memory* (pp. 82–99). Cambridge: Cambridge University Press.

Barclay, C. R., & DeCooke, P. A. (1988). Ordinary everyday memories: Some of the things of which selves are made. In U. Neisser & E. Winograd (Eds.), *Remembering reconsidered: Ecological and traditional approaches to the study of memory* (pp. 91–126). Cambridge: Cambridge University Press.

Barnal, M. (1987). *Black Athena: The Afroasiatic roots of classical civilization.* London: Free Association Books.

Barthes, R. (1975). *S/Z.* London: Cape.

Baudrillard, J. (1983). *Simulacrum & simulation.* Ann Arbor: University of Michigan Press.

Benjamin, W. (1969). The work of art in the age of mechanical reproduction. In *Illuminations: Essays and reflections* (pp. 217–242). New York: Schocken.

Bernard, H. (1995). *Research methods in anthropology: Qualitative and quantitative approaches.* London: Altamira Press.

Bernstein, B. (1977). *Class, codes, and control* (Vol. 3). London: Routledge & Kegan Paul.

Bissell, W. C. (2005). Engaging colonial nostalgia. *Cultural Anthropology, 20*(2), 215–248.

Bourdieu, P. (1984). *Distinction: A social critique of the judgment of taste.* London: Routledge.

Bourdieu, P. (1977). *Outline of a theory of practice.* Cambridge: Cambridge University Press.

Bowles, S., & Gintis, H. (1976). *Schooling in capitalist America.* New York: Basic Books.

Boykin, A. W. (1986). The triple quandary and the schooling of Afro-American children. In U. Neisser (Ed.), *The school achievement of minority children: New perspectives* (pp. 57–92). Hillsdale, NJ: Erlbaum.

Bruce, H. E., & Davis, B. D. (2000). Slam: Hip-hop meets poetry—A strategy for violence intervention. *The English Journal, 89*(5), 119–127.

Buckingham, D., & Sefton-Green, J. (1994). *Cultural studies goes to school: Reading and teaching popular media.* London: Taylor & Francis.

Carter, P. L. (2005). *Keepin' it real: School success beyond Black and White.* Oxford: Oxford University Press.

Clifford, J. (1988). *The predicament of culture: Twentieth-century ethnography, literature, and art.* Cambridge, MA: Harvard University Press.

Clifford, J. (1986). Introduction: Partial truths. In J. Clifford & G. Marcus (Eds.), *Writing culture: The poetics and politics of ethnography* (pp. 1–26). Berkeley and Los Angeles: University of California Press.

Clifford, J., & Marcus, G. (1986). *Writing culture: The poetics and politics of ethnography.* Berkeley and Los Angeles: University of California Press.

Cobb, W. J. (2007). *To the break of dawn: A freestyle on the hip hop aesthetic.* New York: New York University Press.

Cochran-Smith, M., & Lytle, S. L. (2004). Practitioner inquiry, knowledge, and university culture. In J. Loughran, et al., (Eds.), *International handbook of research in self-study of teaching and teacher education practices*. Norwell, MA: Kluwer Publishers.

Cochran-Smith, M., & Lytle, S. L. (1993). *Inside/outside: Teacher research and knowledge*. New York: Teachers College Press.

Condry, I. (2007). *Yellow b-boys, Black culture, and hip-hop in Japan: Toward a transnational cultural politics of race*. Durham, NC: Duke University Press.

Coontz, S. (1992). *The way we never were: American families and the nostalgia trap*. New York: Basic Books.

Cutler, C. (2001). "Keepin it real": White hip-hoppers' discourses of language, race, and authenticity. *Journal of Linguistic Anthropology, 13*(2), 211–233.

Cutwright, P. (1972). The teenage sexual revolution and the myth of an abstinent past. *Family Planning Perspectives, 4*(1), 24–31.

Daspit, T., & Weaver, J. (2001). Critical pedagogy, popular culture, and the creation of meaning. In T. Daspit & J. Weaver (Eds.), *Popular culture and critical pedagogy: A reading, constructing, connecting* (pp. 139–159). New York: Garland.

Davis, M. (1992). *City of quartz: Excavating the future in Los Angeles*. New York: Vintage.

de Certeau, M. (1984). *The practice of everyday life*. Berkeley: University of California Press.

Delgado Bernal, D. (2002). Critical race theory, Latino critical theory, and critical raced-gendered epistemologies: Recognizing students of color as holders and creators of knowledge. *Qualitative Inquiry, 8*(1), 105–126.

Delpit, L. D. (1995). *Other people's children: Cultural conflict in the classroom*. New York: New Press; Distributed by W.W. Norton.

Dey, I. (1993). *Qualitative data analysis: A user-friendly guide for social scientists*. London: Routledge.

Dimitriadis, G. (2001). *Performing identity/performing culture: Hip-hop as text, pedagogy, and lived practice*. New York: Peter Lang.

Dimitriadis, G. (1999). *Popular culture and the boundaries of pedagogy: Constructing selves and social relations at a local community center*. Unpublished book, University of Illnois at Urbana-Champaign.

Dimitriadis, G., & Carlson, D. (2003). Introduction. In G. Dimitriadis & D. Carlson (Eds.), *Promises to keep: Cultural studies, democratic education, and public life* (pp. 1–35). New York: RoutledgeFalmer.

Dimitriadis, G., & McCarthy, C. (2001). *Reading and teaching the postcolonial: From Baldwin to Basquiat and beyond*. New York: Teachers College Press.

Diop, C. A. (1981). *The African origin of civilization: Myth or reality*. New York: Lawrence Hill.

Dixon, T., & Linz, D. (1997). Obscenity law and sexually explicit rap music: Understanding the effect of sex, attitudes and beliefs. *Journal of Applied Communication Research, 25*, 217–241.

Dolby, N. (2001). *Constructing race: Youth, identity, and popular culture in South Africa*. Albany: State University of New York Press.

Dolby, N., & Rizvi, F. (2007). *Youth moves: Identities and education in global perspective*. London & New York: Routledge.

Dumont, J. P. (1978). *The headman and I: Ambiguity and ambivalence in the field-working experience*. Austin: University of Texas Press.

Duncan-Andrade, J., & Morrell, E. (2005). Turn up that radio, teacher: Popular cultural pedagogy in new century urban schools. *Journal of School Leadership, 15*, 284–308.

Dyson, M. E. (2007). *Know what I mean? Reflections on hip hop*. New York: Basic Civitas.

Dyson, M. E. (2005). *Is Bill Cosby right?* New York: Basic Civitas.

Dyson, M. E. (2002). *Open mike*. New York: Basic Civitas.

Dyson, M. E. (2001). *Holler if you hear me: Searching for Tupac Shakur*. New York: Basic Civitas Books.

Dyson, M. E. (2000). *I may not get there with you: The true Martin Luther King Jr.* New York: Free Press

Dyson, M. E. (1996). *Race rules*. New York: Random House.

Dyson, M. E. (1993). *Reflecting Black*. Minneapolis: University of Minnesota Press.

Eagleton, T. (1996). *Literary theory: An introduction*. Minneapolis: University of Minnesota Press.

Earle, J. (2001). Teachers and popular culture consumption. In T. Daspit & J. Weaver (Eds.), *Popular culture and critical pedagogy: A reading, constructing, connecting* (pp. 117–135). New York: Garland.

Ellsworth, E. (1997). *Teaching positions*. New York: Teachers College Press.

Ellsworth, E. (1989). Why doesn't this feel empowering: Working through the repressive myths of critical pedagogy. *Harvard Educational Review, 59*(3), 297–324.

Farber, P., & Holm, G. (1994). A brotherhood of heroes: The charismatic educator in recent American movies. In P. Farber, E. Provenzo, Jr., & G. Holm (Eds.), *Schooling in the light of popular culture*. Albany: State University of New York Press.

Fairclough, N. (2003). *Analyzing discourse: Textual analysis for social research*. London: Routledge.

Fairclough, N. (1985). Critical and descriptive goals in discourse analysis. *Journal of Pragmatics, 9*(6), 739–763.

Farley, C. (2004). What Bill Cosby should be talking about. *Time*. Retrieved May 1, 2005, from http://www.time.com/time/nation/article/0,8599, 645801,00.html

Finders, M. J. (1996). Queens and teen 'zines: Early adolescent females reading their way toward adulthood. *Anthropology and Education Quarterly, 27*(1), 71–89.

Fine, M. (1994). Working the hyphens: Reinventing the self and other in qualitative research. In N. Denzin & Y. Lincoln (Eds.), *Handbook of qualitative research* (pp. 70–82). Newbury Park, CA: Sage.

Fine, M. (1991). *Framing dropouts: Notes on the politics of an urban public high school*. Albany: State University of New York Press.

Fine, M., & Weis, L. (2003). *Silenced voices and extraordinary conversations: Reimagining schools*. New York: Teachers College Press.

Fine, M., Weis, L., Weseen, S., & Wong, L. (2000). For whom? Qualitative research, representations, and social responsibilities. In N. K. Denzin & Y. S. Lincoln (Eds.), *Handbook of qualitative research* (2nd ed., pp. 107–131). Thousand Oaks, CA: Sage.

Fish, S. (1980). *Is there a text in this class? The authority of interpretive communities*. Cambridge, MA: Harvard University Press.

Fiske, J. (1989). *Understanding popular culture*. London: Routledge.

Fiske, J. (1987). *Television culture*. London: Methuen.

Fiske, J. (1979). *Reading television*. London: Routledge.

Fleetwood, N. (2005). Hip-hop fashion, masculine anxiety, & the discourse of Americana. In H. J. Elam & K. A. Jackson (Eds.), *Black cultural traffic: Crossroads in global performance and popular culture* (pp. 326–354). Ann Arbor: University of Michigan Press.

Forman, M. (2002). *The 'hood comes first: Race, space, and place in rap and hip-hop*. Middletown, CT: Wesleyan University Press.

Forman, M. (2005). "Straight outta Mogadishu": Prescribed identities and performative practices among Somali youth in a North American high school. In S. Maira & E. Soep (Eds.), *Youthscapes: The popular, the national, the global* (pp. 3–22). Philadelphia: University of Pennsylvania Press.

Foster, M. (1997). *Black teachers on teaching*. New York: The New Press.

Foucault, M. (1990). *History of sexuality*. New York: Vintage.

Foucault, M. (1977). *Language, counter-memory, practice: Selected essays and interviews*. Ithaca, NY: Cornell University Press.

Freedman, D. (2003). They need someone to show them discipline: Preservice teachers' understandings and expectations of student (re)presentations in *Dangerous Minds*. In G. Dimitriadis & D. Carlson (Eds.), *Promises to keep: Cultural studies, democratic education, and public life* (pp. 245–261). New York: RoutledgeFalmer.

Freire, P., & Macedo, D. (1987). *Literacy: Reading the word & the world*. South Hadley, MA: Bergin & Garvey.

Frith, S. (1998). Defending popular culture from the populists. In J. Storey (Ed.), *Cultural theory & popular culture: A reader* (pp. 570–586). Athens: University of Georgia Press.

Gaunt, K. D. (2006). *The games girls play: Learning the ropes from double-dutch to hip-hop*. New York: New York University Press.

Gates, H. L. (1988). *The signifying monkey*. New York: Oxford.

Gay, G. (2000). *Culturally responsive teaching: Theory, research, and practice*. New York: Teachers College Press.

Ginsburg, F. D., Abu-Lughod, L., & Larkin, B. (2002). *Media worlds: Anthropology on new terrain.* Berkeley and Los Angeles: University of California Press.

Giroux, H. (2004). *The terror of neoliberalism: Authoritarianism and the eclipse of democracy.* Boulder, CO: Paradigm.

Giroux, H. (1997). *Channel surfing: Racism, the media, and the destruction of today's youth.* New York: St. Martin's Press.

Giroux, H. (1996). *Fugitive cultures: Race, violence & youth.* New York: Routledge.

Giroux, H. (1994). *Disturbing pleasures.* New York: Routledge.

Giroux, H. (1992). *Border crossings.* New York: Routledge.

Giroux, H., & McLaren, P. (1989). Schooling, cultural politics and the struggle for democracy. In H. Giroux & P. McLaren (Eds.), *Critical pedagogy, the state, and cultural struggle* (pp. xi–xxv). New York: State University of New York Press.

Giroux, H., & Simon, R. (1989). *Popular culture, schooling, and everyday life.* New York: Bergin & Garvey.

Glaser, B. (1978). *Theoretical sensitivity.* Mill Valley, CA: Sociology Press.

Gore, J. (1998). Disciplining bodies: On the continuity of power relations in pedagogy. In T. Popkewitz & M. Brennan (Eds.), *Foucault's challenge: Discourse, knowledge, and power in education* (pp. 231–255). New York: Teachers College Press.

Gramsci, A. (1971). *Selections from prison notebooks.* New York: International Press.

Griffin, J. (2004). Generations and collective memory revisited: Race, region and memory of civil rights. *American Sociological Review, 69,* 544–557.

Grossberg, L. (1986). Teaching the popular. In C. Nelson (Ed.), *Theory in the classroom* (pp. 177–200). Urbana: University of Illinois Press.

Grossberg, L., Nelson, C., & Treichler, P. (1992). *Cultural studies.* New York: Routledge.

Guinier, L., & Torres, G. (2002). *Miner's canary: Enlisting race, resisting power, transforming democracy.* Cambridge, MA: Harvard University Press.

Gustavson, L. (2002). *Zine writing, graffiti, and turntablism: The creative practices of three youth.* Unpublished doctoral dissertation, University of Pennsylvania.

Halbwachs, M. (1992). *On collective memory.* Chicago: University of Chicago Press.

Hall, P. (1998). The relationship between types of rap music and memory in African American children. *Journal of Black Studies, 28*(6), 802–814.

Hall, S. (1996). The problem of ideology: Marxism without guarantees. In D. Morley & H. Chen (Eds.), *Stuart Hall: Critical dialogues in cultural studies* (pp. 25–46). New York: Routledge.

Healy, C. (2003). Dead man: Film, colonialism, and memory. In R. Hodgkin & S. Radstone (Eds.), *Contested pasts* (pp. 221–236). New York: Taylor & Francis.

Hebdige, D. (1979). *Subculture: The meaning of style.* London: Methuen.

Herzog, H. (1941). On borrowed experience: An analysis of listening to daytime sketches. *Studies in Philosophy and Social Science, 9*(1), 65–95.

Hill, M. L. (in press). Critical pedagogy comes at "halftime": Nas as Black public intellectual. In M. E. Dyson & S. Daulatzai (Eds.), *Reflections on Illmatic 10th anniversary.* New York: BasicCivitas.

Hill, M. L. (2008). Toward a pedagogy of the popular: Bourdieu, hip-hop, and out-of-school literacies. In A. Luke & J. Albright (Eds.), *Bourdieu and literacy education* (pp. 136–161). Mahwah, NJ: Lawrence Erlbaum

Hill, M. L. (2006). Who's representin' for us?: Post-9/11 reflections from Hip-Hop Lit. *English Journal, 96*(5), 25–29.

Hill, M. L. (2005). *(Re)negotiating knowledge, power, and identity in Hip-Hop Lit.* Unpublished doctoral dissertation, University of Pennsylvania

Hill, M. L., Perez, B., & Irby, D. (2008). Street fiction: What is it and what does it mean for English teachers? *English Journal, 97*(3), 76–81.

Hill, M. L., & Vasudevan, L. (Eds.). (2008). *Media, learning, and sites of possibility.* New York: Peter Lang.

Hirsch, M., & Spitzer, L. (2003). We would never have come without you: Generations of nostalgia. In R. Hodgkin & S. Radstone (Eds.), *Contested pasts* (pp. 79–97). New York: Taylor & Francis.

Hodgkin, K., & Radstone, S. (2003). *Contested pasts.* New York: Taylor & Francis.

Holt, G. S. (1999). Stylin' outta the Black pulpit. In G. D. Caponi (Ed.), *Signifyin(g), sanctifyin' & slam dunking: A reader in African American expressive culture* (pp. 331–347). Amherst: University of Massachusetts Press.

hooks, b. (1994). *Outlaw culture: Resisting representations.* New York: Routledge.

Howard, T. C. (2001). Powerful pedagogy for African American students: A case of four teachers. *Urban Education, 36*(179).

Hull, G. (1993). Critical literacy and beyond: Lessons learned from students and workers in a vocational program and on the job. *Anthropology and Education Quarterly, 24,* 308–317.

Hull, G., & Schultz, K. (2002). *School's out! Bridging out-of-school literacies with classroom practice.* New York: Teachers College Press.

Huyssen, A. (2000). Present pasts: Media, politics, amnesia. *Public Culture, 12*(1), 21–28.

Huyssen, A. (1994). *Twilight memories: Marking time in a culture of amnesia.* New York: Routledge.

Hytten, K. (1999). The promise of culture studies in education. *Educational Theory, 49*(4), 527–543.

Hymes, D. (1974). *Foundations in sociolinguistics: An ethnographic approach.* Philadelphia: University of Pennsylvania Press.

Hymes, D. (1972). *Reinventing anthropology.* New York: Vintage.

Ibrahim, A. (1999). Becoming Black: Rap and hip-hop, race gender, identity and the politics of ESL learning. *TESOL Quarterly, 15*(3), 349–369.

Jackson, J. (2005). *Real Black: Adventures in racial sincerity.* Chicago: University of Chicago Press.

Jackson, P. (1968). *Life in classrooms* New York: Holt, Rinehart, & Winston.

James, G. (1954). *Stolen legacy: Greek philosophy is stolen Egyptian philosophy.* Lawrenceville, NJ: Africa World Press.

Johnson, E. P. (2003). *Appropriating Blackness: Performance and the politics of authenticity.* Durham, NC: Duke University Press.

Johnson, J. D., Jackson, L. A., & Gatto, L. (1995). Violent attitudes and deferred academic aspirations: Deleterious effects of exposure to rap music. *Basic and Applied Social Psychology, 16*(1), 27–41.

Kamberelis, G., & Dimitriadis, G. (2005). *On qualitative inquiry.* New York: Teachers College Press.

Kaplan, A. (2003). Homeland insecurities: Some reflections on language and space. *Radical History Review, 85,* 82–93.

Kelley, R. (1998). *Yo mama's disfunktional: Fighting the culture wars in urban America.* Boston: Beacon.

Kellner, D. (2000). Multiple literacies and critical pedagogies: New paradigms. In P. Trifonas (Ed.), *Revolutionary pedagogies: Cultural politics, instituting education, and the discourse of theory* (pp. 196–221). New York: Routledge.

Kellner, D. (1998). *Boundaries and borderlines: Reflections on Jean Baudrillard and critical theory.* Retrieved on May 4, 2005, from http://www.uta.edu/huma/illuminations/kell2.htm

Kellner, D. (1995). *Media culture: Cultural studies, identity and politics between the modern and the postmodern.* New York: Routledge.

Kellner, D. (1992). Toward a multiperspectival cultural studies. *Centennial Review, 26*(1), 5–41.

Kitwana, B. (2002). *The hip-hop generation: Young Blacks and the crisis in African-American culture.* New York: Basic Civitas.

Krims, A. (2000). *Rap music and the poetics of identity.* Cambridge: Cambridge University Press.

Ladson-Billings, G. (1998). Just what is critical race theory and what's it doing in a nice field like education? *Qualitative Studies in Education, 11,* 7–24.

Ladson-Billings, G. (1994). *The dreamkeepers: Successful teachers of African-American children.* San Francisco: Jossey-Bass.

Lather, P. (1993). Fertile obsession: Validity after poststructuralism. *Sociological Quarterly, 34,* 673–693.

Lather, P. (1986). Research as praxis. *Harvard Educational Review, 56,* 257–277.

Lee, C. D. (1995a). A culturally based cognitive apprenticeship: Teaching African American high school students skills in literary interpretation. *Reading Research Quarterly, 30*(40), 608–631.

Lee, C. D. (1995b). The use of signifying as a scaffold for literary interpretation. *Journal of Black Psychology, 21*(4), 357–381.

Lee, C. D. (1993). *Signifying as a scaffold for literary interpretation: The pedagogical implications of an African American discourse genre* (Research Report Series). Urbana, IL: National Council of Teachers of English.

Lee, C. D., Spencer, M. B., & Harpalani, V. (2003). "Every shut eye ain't sleep": Studying how people live culturally. *Educational Researcher, 32*(5), 6–13.

Lefkowitz, M. R. (1996). *Not out of Africa: How Afrocentrism became an excuse to teach myth as history.* New York: Basic.

Leonard, J., & Hill, M. L. (2008). Using culturally relevant texts to facilitate classroom science discourse. *Journal of Black Studies, 39*(1), 22–42.

Lévi-Strauss, C. (1966). *The savage mind.* Chicago: University of Chicago Press.

Lincoln, C. E. (1973). *Black Muslims in America.* Lawrenceville, NJ: Red Sea Press.

Lipsitz, G. (1992). *Time passages: Collective memory and American popular culture.* Minneapolis: University of Minnesota Press.

Lowenthal, L. (1961). *Literature, popular culture and society.* Englewood Cliffs, NJ: Prentice-Hall.

Luke, C. (1997). Media literacy and cultural studies. In S. Muspratt, A. Luke, & P. Freebody (Eds.), *Constructing critical literacies: Teaching and learning textual practice* (pp. 19–49). Cresskill, NJ: Hampton Press.

Lukose, R. (2007). The children of liberalization: Youth agency and globalization in India. In N. Dolby & F. Rizvi (Eds.), *Youth moves: Identities and education in global perspective* (pp. 133–150). New York: Routledge.

Maanen, J. (1995). *Representation in ethnography.* Thousand Oaks, CA: Sage.

Mahiri, J. (1998). *Shooting for excellence.* New York: Teachers College Press.

Maxwell, J. (1996). *Qualitative research design: An interactive approach.* Thousand Oaks, CA: Sage.

McCloud, A. (1995). *African American Islam.* New York: Routledge.

McGuigan, J. (1992). *Cultural populism.* London: Routledge.

McLaren, P. (1999). Gangsta pedagogy and ghettocentricity: The hip-hop nation as counter-public sphere. In C. McCarthy, G. Hudak, S. Miklaucic, & P. Saukko (Eds.), *Sound identities: Popular music and the cultural politics of education* (pp. 19–64). New York: Peter Lang.

McLaren, P. (1989). *Life in schools: An introduction to critical pedagogy in the foundations of education.* New York: Longman.

McWhorter, J. (2001). *Losing the race: Self sabotage in Black America.* New York: HarperCollins.

Miles, M. B., & Huberman, A. M. (1994). *Qualitative data analysis: An expanded sourcebook* (2nd ed.). Thousand Oaks, CA: Sage.

Miyakawa, F. (2003). *God hop: The music and message of five percenter rap.* Unpublished doctoral dissertation, Indiana University, Bloomington.

Moll, L. C., & Greenberg, J. (1990). Creating zones of possibilities: Combining social contexts for instruction. In L. C. Moll (Ed.), *Vygotsky and education* (pp. 319–348). Cambridge: Cambridge University Press.

Moores, S. (1993). *Interpreting audiences: The ethnography of media consumption.* London: Routledge.

Morley, D. (1992). *Television, audiences and cultural studies.* London: Routledge.

Morrell, E. (2002). Toward a critical pedagogy of popular culture: Literacy development among urban youth. *Journal of Adolescent & Adult Literacy, 46*(1), 72–77.

Morrell, E., & Duncan-Andrade, J. M. R. (2002). Promoting academic literacy with urban youth through engaging in hip-hop culture. *English Journal, 91*(6), 88–92.

Murdock, G. (1997). Cultural studies at the crossroads. In A. McRobbie (Ed.), *Back to reality? Social experience and cultural studies* (pp. 58–73). Manchester, UK: Manchester University Press.

Nietzsche, F. (1969). *Genealogy of morals.* New York: Random House.

Nora, P. (1996). *Realms of memory.* New York: Columbia University Press.

Olick, J. K. (1999). Collective memory: The two cultures. *Sociological Theory, 17*(3), 333–348.

Omi, M., & Winant, H. (1994). *Racial formation in the United States: From the 1960s to the 1990s.* New York: Routledge.

O'Reilly, M. R. (1993). *The peaceable classroom.* Portsmouth, NH: Boynton/Cook.

Ortner, S. B. (2006). *Anthropology and social theory: Culture, power, and the acting subject.* Durham, NC: Duke University Press.

Osumare, H. (2007). *The Africanist aesthetic in global hip-hop: Power moves.* New York: Palgrave Macmillan.

Pardue, D. (2004). "Writing in the margins": Brazilian hip-hop as an educational project. *Anthropology & Education Quarterly, 35*(4), 411–432.

Pearson, R. (1999). Custer loses again: The contestation over commodified cultural memory. In D. Ben-Amos & D. Weissberg (Eds.), *Cultural memory and the construction of identity* (pp. 176–201). Detroit, MI: Wayne State University Press.

Pennycook, A. (2005). Teaching with the flow: Fixity and fluidity in education. *Asia Pacific Journal of Education, 25*(1), 29–43.

Perry, I. (2004). *Prophets of the hood: Politics and poetics in hip hop.* Durham, NC: Duke University Press.

Petchauer, E. M. (in press). Knowing what's up and learning what you're not supposed to: Critical consciousness among hip-hop collegians. *Lincoln Journal of Social and Political Thought.*

Pollock, M. (2004). *Colormute: Race talk dilemmas in an American school.* Princeton, NJ: Princeton University Press.

Pompe, C. (1996). But they're pink!—Who cares!: Popular culture in the primary years. In M. Hilton (Ed.), *Potent fictions: Children's literacy and the challenge of popular culture* (pp. 92–125). London: Routledge.

Pough, G. (2004). *Check it while I wreck it: Black womanhood, hip-hop culture, and the public sphere.* New York: Columbia University Press.

Powell, C. T. (1991). Rap music: An education with a beat from the street. *Journal of Negro Education, 60*(3), 245–259.

Pratt, M. L. (1986). Fieldwork in common places. In J. Clifford & G. Marcus (Eds.), *Writing culture: The poetics and politics of ethnography* (pp. 27–50). Berkeley: University of California Press.

Quinn, E. (2005). *Nuthin' but a "G" thang: The culture and commerce of gangsta rap*. New York: Columbia University Press.

Radway, J. (1991). *Reading the romance: Women, patriarchy, and the modern romance*. Chapel Hill, NC: University of North Carolina Press.

Rice, J. (2003). The 1963 hip-hop machine: Hip-hop pedagogy as composition. *College Composition and Communication, 54*(3), 453–471.

Richardson, L. (2000). Writing: A method of inquiry. In N. K. Denzin & Y. S. Lincoln (Eds.), *Handbook of qualitative research* (2nd ed., pp. 923–948). Thousand Oaks, CA: Sage.

Rivera, R. Z. (2003). *New York Ricans from the Hip Hop Zone*. New York: Palgrave Macmillan.

Roberts, J. W. (1989). *From trickster to badman: The Black folk here in slavery and freedom*. Philadelphia: University of Pennsylvania Press.

Robertson, S. (1990). Text rendering: Beginning literary response. *English Journal, 79*(1), 80–84.

Robinson, M. (1997). *Children reading print and television*. London: Falmer.

Rogers, J. (1986). Dictionary of clichés. New York: Ballantine.

Roman, L. G., & Apple, M. W. (1990). Is naturalism a move away from positivism? Materialist and feminist approaches to subjectivities in ethnographic research. In E. W. Eisner & A. Peshkin (Eds.), *Qualitative inquiry in education: The continuing debate* (pp. 38–73). New York: Teachers College Press.

Rosaldo, R. (1989). *Culture and truth: The remaking of social analysis*. Boston: Beacon.

Rose, T. (1994). *Black noise: Rap music and Black culture in contemporary America*. Middletown, CT: Wesleyan University Press.

Said, E. (1979). *Orientalism*. New York: Vintage.

Samuel, R. (1994). *Theatres of memory: Past and present in contemporary culture*. London: Verso.

Saussure, F. (1972). Course in general linguistics. In R. DeGeorge & F. DeGeorge (Eds.), *The structuralists from Marx to Lévi-Strauss* (pp. 59–79). Garden City, NY: Anchor.

School District of Philadelphia. (2003). *Howard High School Handbook*. Philadelphia, PA: Author.

Schultz, K. (2003). *Listening: A framework for teaching across difference*. New York: Teachers College Press.

Schwartz, B. (1991). Iconography and collective memory: Lincoln's image in the American mind. *The sociological quarterly, 32*(3), 301–319.

Sharpley-Whiting, T. D. (2007). *Pimps up, hoes down: Hip-hop's hold on young Black women*. New York: New York University Press.

Sherman, D. J. (1999). *The construction of memory in interwar France*. Chicago: Chicago University Press.

Silverman, K. (1999). *The threshold of the visible world*. New York: Routledge.

Slavin, R. E. (1990). Research on cooperative learning: Consensus and controversy. *Educational Leadership, 47*(4), 52–54.

Slavin, R. E., & Oickle, E. M. (1981). Effects of cooperative learning teams on student achievement and race relations: Treatment by race interactions. *Sociology of Education, 54*(3), 174–180.

Sleeter, C. (2001). An analysis of the critiques of multicultural education. In J. A. Banks & C. A. McGee Banks (Eds.), *Handbook of research on multicultural education* (pp. 81–94). New York: Jossey-Bass.

Smith, P. (2000). Rethinking Joe: Exploring the borders of *Lean on Me*. In T. Daspit & J. A. Weaver (Eds.), *Popular culture and critical pedagogy: Reading, constructing, connecting* (pp. 3–31). New York: Garland.

Smitherman, G. (1977). *Talkin and testifyin: The language of Black America.* Detroit: Wayne University Press.

Spitzer, L. (1998). *Hotel Bolivia: The culture of memory in a refuge from Nazism.* New York: Hill and Wang.

Stovall, D. (2006). Hip-hop culture, critical pedagogy, and the urban classroom. *Urban Education, 41*(6), 585–602.

Swedenburg, T. (2004). Homies in the 'hood: Rap's commodification of insubordination. In M. Forman & M. A. Neal (Eds.), *That's the joint: The hip-hop studies reader* (pp. 579–592). New York: Routledge.

Thomas, D. (2004). *Modern Blackness: Nationalism, globalization, and the politics of culture in Jamaica.* Durham, NC: Duke University Press.

Thompson, J. B. (1990). *Ideology and modern culture: Critical social theory in the era of mass communication.* Cambridge: Polity.

Took, K. J., & Weiss, D. S. (1994). The relationship between heavy metal and rap music on adolescent turmoil: Real or artifact? In *Adolescence, 29,* 613–621.

Trofanenko, B. (2006). Displayed object, indigenous identities, and public pedagogy. *Anthropology & Education Quarterly, 37*(4), 309–327.

Trouillot, M. (1995). *Silencing the past: Power and the production of history.* Boston: Beacon.

Tyson, E. H. (2002). Hip hop therapy: An exploratory study of a rap music intervention with at-risk and delinquent youth. *Journal of Poetry Therapy, 15*(3), 131–144.

Van Maanen, J. (1995). An end to innocence: The ethnography of ethnography. In J. van Maanen (Ed.), *Representation in ethnography* (pp. 1–21). Thousand Oaks, CA: Sage.

Weis, L., & Fine, M. (2000). *Construction sites: Excavating race, class, and gender among urban youth.* New York: Teachers College Press.

Weiss, J. (2000). *To have and to hold: Marriage, the baby boom, and social change.* Chicago and London: University of Chicago Press.

Weiss, M. (2003). Great expectations: Baby boomer wealth forecasts wilt. *American Demographics, 25*(4), 26–35.

Wertsch, J. (2002). *Voices of collective remembering.* Cambridge: Cambridge University Press.

West, C. (1993). *Race matters.* New York: Beacon.

Index

About the Author

Marc Lamont Hill is Associate Professor of English Education and Anthropology at Teachers College, Columbia University. He has published in journals such as *Teachers College Record, English Journal, International Journal of Qualitative Studies in Education,* and *Journal of Black Studies.* His research interests include anthropology of education, ethnography of reading, youth culture, masculinity, globalization, and African American literacies. In addition to his scholarly work, he is a social activist and organizer.